THE NECESSITY OF CHRIST IN THE LIFE OF A WOMAN

THE NECESSITY OF CHRIST IN THE LIFE OF A WOMAN

31 DAY DEVOTIONAL

Allison Johnson

To my husband who I would marry all over again - thank you for our journey.

To Pastor, Reverend Frederick C. Johnson
Under your teaching, you always left me wanting to increase in knowledge, wisdom, and understanding to know more about this wonderful Savior, as you opened your Bible studies with the question, "What do you want to know?"

To all the women who want to dig deeper and finish well to the glory of God.

Who desires to know
Jesus the Christ
to love Him more
to serve Him more
-

"I press toward the goal for the prize of the upward call of God in Christ Jesus. Therefore let us, as many as are mature, have this mind; and if in anything you think otherwise, God will reveal even this to you." Philippians 3:14-15

TABLE OF CONTENTS

FOREWORD BY FIRST LADY

This devotional, written in 2017 by First Baptist Church of Glenarden's (FBCG) very own Allison Johnson, will deepen your understanding of who God is while igniting a fire to share Christ with the world! In a time when the message of Jesus is being challenged by human intellect and opinions, when truth is no longer rooted in the word of God, we are called to reflect the authenticity of Christ. That year, the FBCG Women's Group sought to challenge women to *know* what they Believe, to boldly *articulate* what they believe and to have the ability to confidently *defend* what they BELIEVE.

I sense that we are living in the last days and God is demanding His children to share the core message of love, hope and redemption. I am confident that after you spend 31 days in this devotional, you will turn the last page, close the book and open your heart to share with the world what you BELIEVE.

The church must make an impact for Christ, and we as women can be the catalyst! Jesus is the answer and we are the conduits between the needs of this world and the solution. Do you BELIEVE?

First Lady Trina Jenkins
Chief Ministry Officer
First Baptist Church of Glenarden International

PREFACE

I sat in a director's meeting in April of 2017 when First Lady Trina Jenkins began to discuss her vision for the ladies for the upcoming year. She wanted the First Baptist Church of Glenarden (FBCG) ladies to know Christ better and to think theologically about Him. As I listened, everything in me echoed her passion and heart for women to go beyond the surface and "know" the Christ of the scriptures. Her desire touched a cord in my soul because it was aligned with my life's purpose to see the body of Christ dig deeper into theology and grow so that it can finish well for the Glory of God. Her passion and desire that our devotional for 2018 would draw and lead the women of our congregation to go deeper into Christ was a symphony to my ears.

Each January, the women of FBCG, under the leadership of our First Lady, begin the year with fasting, prayer, and a devotional that unites and centers us for the year ahead. It anchors us in who we are in Christ and how we can develop deeper as dynamic disciples. This yearly discipleship practice creates discipline and duplication from our lives to the lives of others. It sets the foundational stamina for the upcoming year's opportunities, challenges, and triumphs.

As First Lady Trina continued to paint the picture for the fourteen directors around the long boardroom conference table, she excitedly discussed Lee Strobel's book and how it would be great to have a devotional highlighting "The Case for Christ." I was one of the few at the table familiar with Lee Strobel's work and an alumna of the Trinity Evangelical Divinity School seminary in Deerfield, IL. So, as I surveyed the room and listened to her heart for the ladies, and knowing how I enjoyed every Systematic Theology course I took in school, I wanted to volunteer to research how we could bring the vision to fruition. So, without hesitation, I offered to investigate how to make her vision occur. Two other fellow directors immediately stepped forward to assist with this endeavor, and we became the committee for the 2018 devotional.

During the next month, I immersed myself in "The Case for Christ." I outlined the book's content and realized that if we were going to write a 21-day devotional for the women of our congregation based on "The Case for Christ," we would need all sorts of permissions. I knew we didn't have the time to gain approval, so while 30,000 feet above the clouds, on my way to Indianapolis, Indiana, in the spring of 2017, I wondered what we could do. In what ways could I write a theological devotional about Christ that captured First Lady's vision and passionate heart? As I peered out at the blue sky and considered the outline, with a blue pen in hand, the five sections in the devotional you now hold flowed onto my 8x11 pad with the gracious help of the Holy Spirit. Over the next couple of months, the design, content outline, and proposal submission received enthusiastic approval from First Lady Trina. Providence would have it that in September 2017, I would transition from a ten-year subcontracting senior instructor position and have the time to devote my full attention to the "Necessity of Christ in the Life of a Woman, 2018 Women's Devotional and Believe Fast."

As I wrote, Sherry Saylor, Director of Divine Discipleship for Women, was a motivating and guiding light. When I told her what I thought the title should be, she immediately confirmed with excitement exclaiming, "Yes, yes, we need to know how necessary Christ is in our lives." When I shared with her a week later that I had begun writing the 21-day devotional, she informed me frankly and lovingly that January had 31 days, so the devotional needed to cover the entire month. Are you sure it must be thirty-one days? I questioned. I was sure we only had a 21-day devotional the year prior. To which she responded - absolutely! We need a devotional for each day in January. I dutifully added ten more devotional topics, which I now know provide a fuller theological picture of how necessary Christ is in our lives as women.

Jackie Parker, the Director of the Women's Focus Studies, is the third person on our committee. She provided institutional knowledge as she had participated in the January Women's devotional and fasts for many years. Once hearing the title, she too affirmed how the title aligned with the First Lady's vision. Throughout the writing of this project, Jackie encouraged, supported, and kept the looming deadline before me to ensure we finished before Thanksgiving. Her implicit timekeeping skills had me rehearsing the line from the Apollo 13 movie, "Failure is not an option." It was a blessing to have Jackie's years of knowledge that allowed this book to enter editing, marketing, and advertising by the second week of November 2017.

Our Senior Editor and book designer, Angela Hendrix Bell, with her editors Chandra Carriere Young, Grace Magazine Editor, Verna Smith, Grace Magazine Copy Editor, and Taunya Sills, Grace Magazine Proofreader, did a masterful job in making the Necessity of Christ in the Life of a Woman, 2018 Women's Devotional and Believe Fast, ready by the final week in December for download and participation.

Partnering with Grace Magazine's Senior Editor was a team of FBCG's Spanish Ministry members. The translators ensured this devotional's meaning and accuracy were never lost in each deadline of edits. Through the dedication and sleepless nights of Cleo Pecou, Sholem Cox, Rhonda Wright, and Diana Alvares, they amazingly produced La Necesidad De Cristo En La Vida De Una Mujer El Devocional para Mujeres y Ayuno de Creer Del 2018 2da Edicion.

Unbeknownst to me, in mid-December, the stellar marketing team who spent countless hours ensuring that the devotional met the standard of excellence FBCG is known for made a grammatical change to week one, day four, which added the conjunction "or" for grammatical correctness. The correction changed the Trinity to modalism, a heresy fought throughout church history and with us today. From my seminary training and life as a Bible teacher, I know that the wrong conjunction, preposition, or article can change theological accuracy. Since some ladies downloaded the first edition before I discovered the error, a second edition was published to maintain the theological accuracy of the Trinity, which is God in three persons and not God in three modes like a child's transformer toy that morphs into a different figure.

The final participation data for the devotional you now hold was experienced on average by over 997 fasting and praying women who joined the live 5:30

am conference calls or recordings each weekday in January 2018. Shortly after completing this devotional, we implemented a six-week 90-minute Bible study at the First Baptist Church of Glenarden, where women dug, unpacked, and mined the scriptures in the Deeper Still section for additional theological insights. These women shared their thoughts and application as they embraced how necessary Christ is in their lives.

I am honored to present a theological understanding of why Christ is necessary for a woman's life. I am eternally grateful for First Lady Trina Jenkins, who commissioned this book through leadership, passion, and vision in that evening meeting of Directors in the spring of 2017.

As I went to publishing, I shortened the title to "The Necessity of Christ in the Life of a Woman." I want this devotional to connect you and challenge you to dig deeper, so I omitted FBCG-specific tutorials on prayer and fasting that were part of the original manuscripts.

May the question I asked on the way to Indiana, 30,000 feet above the clouds, bring you a more excellent knowledge of Christ. May it help you persevere and finish well to the Glory of God!

INTRODUCTION

As you embark on this journey, my hope and trust is that this devotional will deepen your theology and your appreciation for Jesus, the Christ, the Son of the True and Living God.

During the next 31 days, we will examine who Jesus is and why He matters. If Christ is truly necessary in the life of a woman, then we must have a desire to know Him, the power of His resurrection and the fellowship of His sufferings, being conformed to His death (Philippians 3:10, NKJV)[1].

Definition

Theology comes from a combination of two Greek words: theos, which means God, and logos, which means reason, wisdom or thought. Literally, then theology means "God-thought" or "reasoning about God." Some dictionaries define it more formally and specifically as "the science of God," but science in this sense simply means "reflection on something." So at its most basic level, theology is any thinking, reflecting or contemplating on the reality of God—even on the question of God. (Grenz, 1996)

PURPOSE

This devotional was written for the women of First Baptist Church of Glenarden and beyond. It is my desire that each woman will deepen her theology and appreciation for Jesus, the Christ. This devotional is not meant to scratch the surface, but to draw you deeper in your faith. While I attempted to keep each devotional as short as possible and focused, my hope is that you will gain a greater depth and breadth of understanding of the Savior as you encounter the scriptures each day. I pray you will think and reflect on what each scripture means about Him. My purpose is that you believe and understand what the Bible has to say about this wonderful Savior and that you will tell those who cross your path why you BELIEVE in the person and deity of Jesus, the Christ.

---

[1] All scripture references in this devotional are from the New King James Version (NKJV).

GOALS

My goals are:

1. to provide you with topics and scriptures which will enhance your knowledge of Jesus Christ now and in years to come,

2. to encourage you to dig and highlight scriptures,

3. to inspire you to read notes in a good study Bible with commentary for a deeper understanding of the text,

4. to equip the woman of God who holds this devotional with a solid Biblical foundation to **Share** Christ, **Stand** for Christ and **Stay** in Christ's presence in order to win souls to Jesus, and

For you to be equipped, strengthened, fortified and on fire about leading others to Him!

OVERVIEW

"The Necessity of Christ in the Life of a Woman" will be a rich journey and it will also challenge you to dig into the Word of God. I want you to learn, confirm, validate and strengthen what you know and believe about Jesus. We want Jesus to be in the forefront of all that you do this year and frankly, for the rest of your life.

Each week, we will study and examine different aspects of Jesus. In week one, we will focus on answering the question *Who Is Christ?* In week two, we explore the question *Why Is Christ Important?* How Jesus is unique and His impact on the lives of women in the Gospels will be our central focus in our third week. Week four, "Compelled to Tell about My Jesus!" will bring together all that we are learning and challenges us to tell others while maintaining a tri-fold tension of love, compassion and truth. Finally, week five challenges us to assess our current walk in Christ and beckons us to Cling to the Savior! On those days that you have more time, you will find the Deeper Still section enriching as it expands your Biblical knowledge of the concepts taught in that day's reading.

Make sure you allocate enough time to spend time in the Word of God each day. You are encouraged not to skip the main body of scriptures for the daily reading; they will lead you to the central purpose and goal for that day. Pray now that God will equip you to go the distance.

HELPFUL TOOLS

Recommended Study Bibles

NKJV Study Bible
The John MacArthur Study Bible (NKJV, NASB, ESV)
The Thompson Chain-Reference Study Bible (NKJV)
Life Application Study Bible (NKJV)

Christ's Devotional Life (Thompson, p. 1903, Ref. No 2834)

"And when He had sent the multitudes away, He went up on the mountain by Himself to pray. Now when evening came, He was alone there." (Matthew 14:23)

"Then Jesus came with them to a place called Gethsemane, and said to the disciples, Sit here while I go and pray over there." (Matthew 26:36)

"He went a little farther and fell on His face, and prayed, saying, 'O My Father, if it is possible, let this cup pass from Me; nevertheless, not as I will, but as You will.'"

(Matthew 26:39)

"Again, a second time, He went away and prayed, saying, 'O My Father, if this cup cannot pass away from Me unless I drink it, Your will be done.'" (Matthew 26:42)

"Now in the morning, having risen a long while before daylight, He went out and departed to a solitary place; and there he prayed." (Mark 1:35)

"And when He had sent them away, He departed to the mountain to pray. Now when evening came, the boat was in the middle of the sea; and He was alone on the land."

(Mark 6:46-47)

"Again He went away and prayed, and spoke the same words." (Mark 14:39)

"Now it came to pass, about eight days after these sayings, that He took Peter, John and James and went up on the mountain to pray." (Luke 9:28)

Salvation Scripture Map

John 3:16
"For God so loved the world that He gave His only begotten Son, that whoever believes in Him should not perish but have everlasting life."

ROMANS ROAD
Romans 3:10
"As it is written: 'There is none righteous, no, not one;'"

Romans 3:23
"for all have sinned and fall short of the glory of God,"

Romans 5:12
"Therefore, just as through one man sin entered the world, and death through sin, and thus death spread to all men, because all sinned"

Romans 5:8
"But God demonstrates His own love toward us in that while we were still sinners, Christ died forus."

Romans 6:23
"For the wages of sin is death, but the gift of God is eternal life in Christ Jesus our Lord."

Romans 10:9-10
"that if you confess with your mouth the Lord Jesus and believe in your heart that God has raised Him from the dead, you will be saved. For with the heart one believes unto righteousness, and with the mouth confession is made unto salvation."

Romans 10:13
For "whoever calls on the name of the LORD shall be saved."

Prayer of Repentance

Heavenly Father, I come to you in the name of Jesus, the Son of the one true God. I need Jesus Christ to save me from Hell's fire and an eternal life without you. I confess that I am a sinner in need of the Lord Jesus. I believe in my heart that God raised Jesus from the dead. Now Lord, please cleanse me and save me from my sins according to your grace through my faith in whom You are and the provisions Jesus Christ made on the cross. I pray this in accordance with Romans 10:9-10 and Ephesians 2:8-10. In Jesus' name, amen.

Prayer of Rededication

Heavenly Father, I come to you in the name of Jesus Christ. I acknowledge that I have turned my back on you. I have been busy doing my own thing and not treating you as Lord of my life. I have been living beneath my heavenly inheritance of eternal life. Father, forgive me of my sins. I stand on your promise according to 1 John 1:9-10. Cleanse me right now of all unrighteousness. Thank you, Lord, for forgiving me. I pray this not to be saved, I pray this because I am saved and you are a forgiving father to me, your child. In Jesus' name, amen.

Week 1: Who is Christ?

"If you want to see God,
look at Jesus Christ."
~Billy Graham

IS JESUS YOUR KING?

1 Timothy 6:13-16

Your natural reaction to the question above, is most likely, "yes, of course He's my King." But when was the last time you stopped to consider what you know and think about Jesus Christ? For the next 31 days, we will think and meditate on who Jesus is in our lives, today. The truth is, many only think of Him as a distant memory connected to their salvation experience. In these next few weeks, we are going to dig and examine who Christ is to us and why He is important. Next, we will consider those around us and we will be challenged to take our love for the Savior to the streets! So, let's begin our journey by examining just a few things about Jesus.

"My King" is a popular portion of a sermon, delivered in Detroit in 1976, by the late Dr. S.M. Lockridge, former Pastor of Calvary Baptist Church, in San Diego. You may want to hear the audio version on YouTube as you read along.[2] The point is to examine and ask yourself, *Where is Christ in my life? Is Christ seated on the throne in my life or has someone else snuck up there?*

My King[3]

- The Bible says my king is the King of the Jews.
- He's the King of Israel.
- He's the King of Righteousness.
- He's the King of the Ages.
- He's the King of Heaven.
- He's the King of Glory.
- He's the King of Kings, and He's the Lord of Lords.
- That's my King.

I wonder if you know Him.

- My King is a sovereign King.
- No means of measure can define His limitless love.
- He's enduringly strong.
- He's entirely sincere.
- He's eternally steadfast.
- He's immortally graceful.
- He's imperially powerful.
- He's impartially merciful.

---

[2] S.M. Lockridge. "That's My King," uploaded by Albert Martin, July 23, 2008, YouTube sermon video, 3:18, https://www.youtube.com/watch?v=yzqTFNfeDnE.

[3] S.M. Lockridge, "That's My King," accessed June 15, 2023, https://thatsmyking.wordpress.com/words

Do you know Him?

- He's the greatest phenomenon that has ever crossed the horizon of this world.
- He's God's Son.
- He's the sinner's Savior.
- He's the centerpiece of civilization.
- He's unparalleled.
- He's unprecedented.
- He is the loftiest idea in literature.
- He's the highest personality in philosophy.
- He's the fundamental doctrine of true theology.
- He's the only one qualified to be an all-sufficient Savior.

I wonder if you know Him today.

- He supplies strength for the weak.
- He's available for the tempted and the tried.
- He sympathizes and He saves.
- He strengthens and sustains.
- He guards and He guides.
- He heals the sick.
- He cleansed the lepers.
- He forgives sinners.
- He discharges debtors.
- He delivers the captive.
- He defends the feeble.
- He blesses the young.
- He serves the unfortunate.
- He regards the aged.
- He rewards the diligent.

And He beautifies the meek.

- I wonder if you know Him.
- He's the key to knowledge.
- He's the wellspring of wisdom.
- He's the doorway of deliverance.
- He's the pathway of peace.
- He's the roadway of righteousness.
- He's the highway of holiness.
- He's the gateway of glory.

Do you know Him? Well ...

- His life is matchless.
- His goodness is limitless.
- His mercy is everlasting.
- His love never changes.
- His word is enough.

- His grace is sufficient.
- His reign is righteous.
- And His yoke is easy.
- And His burden is light.

I wish I could describe Him to you. Yes ...

- He's indescribable!
- He's incomprehensible.
- He's invincible.
- He's irresistible.
- You can't get Him out of your mind.
- You can't get Him off of your hand.
- You can't outlive Him, and you can't live without Him.
- Well, the Pharisees couldn't stand Him, but they found out they couldn't stop Him.
- Pilate couldn't find any fault in Him.
- Herod couldn't kill Him.
- Death couldn't handle Him and the grave couldn't hold Him.

Yeah! That's my King, that's my King.

Amen!

Wow! As you listened to or read and considered Dr. Lockridge's points on the kingship of Christ and as you think about Paul's writing to Timothy, what is your conclusion? Who is Christ to you?

Time to Reflect

Scripture: 1 Timothy 6:13-16

Observation: What are some of your thoughts and feelings?

Application: What can you start, stop or continue doing? How can you apply this to your life?

Prayer: Pray about any <u>one</u> of the suggested options below. You are not expected to do all three unless the Holy Spirit directs you otherwise.

What can you commit to Jesus?
What do you want Him to do for you?
What do you want Him to help you to do?

Deeper Still: Using a good study Bible with commentary, review the following Scriptures concerning Christ's Divinity as King of Kings: *Deut. 10:17; Josh. 22:22; Ps. 24:7; 72:11; 136:3; Zech. 6:5; Rev. 1:5; 17:14; 19:12, 16.*

Praise and Worship: What praise or worship song comes to mind as you conclude our devotional for the day? I encourage you to listen to it now. Below is my playlist, which has a variety of artists and genres, so hold on and enjoy it if you care to partake.

"Behold Our God" – Shiloh Church Choir[4]
"Worthy of it All" – CeCe Winans[5]

---

[4] The Shiloh Church Choir, "Behold Our God [Lyric Video]," Sovereign Grace Music together with The Shiloh Church Choir, uploaded by Sovereign Grace Music, October 29, 2019, YouTube music video, 6:50, https://www.youtube.com/watch?v=lIUGUPEopbI.

[5] CeCe Winans, "Worthy of it All (Official Audio)," uploaded by CeCe Winans, March 12, 2021, YouTube music video, 5:28, https://www.youtube.com/watch?v=JzZSrOPeoIc.

THE GREATEST STORY EVER TOLD

Isaiah 9:6-7a

Don't you just love a good story? A story that has a main character who is the underdog or facing some type of insurmountable obstacle? In a really good story, you're biting your nails and wondering, *how is the person going to get out of this?* There appears to be no way the character can escape and get out or overcome the situation. She has no apparent resources to fight or win. Drama, suspense, intrigue, thrills, a touch of comedy and a few twists have you on the edge of your seat. Then, the unimaginable happens. The person musters the necessary resources to fight back, wins and lives happily ever after. Or better yet, a hero arises and saves the day for her to live happily ever after. You close your book or leave the movie and think, *Wow! Why doesn't something like that happen for me?* Well there is really good news: in the greatest story ever told, you are the main character. Yes, that's right, little ole you.

As the main character of our own story, we all begin as the underdog, we are defeated and slaves to sin. We have Adam and Eve to thank for this (Genesis 3: 1-19). But hold on, make no mistake, not one of us will be able to stand on the Day of Judgment and blame God, Adam or Eve for our sin. Proverbs 5:22 says, *"His own iniquities entrap the wicked man, and he is caught in the cords of his sin."* Paul writes in Romans 3:23, *"For all have sinned and fall short of the glory of God."*

In our own story, like in Genesis 3, we have that same pernicious obstacle and villain, Satan himself, who comes to kill, steal and destroy (John 10:10). We cooperate with him until the Father, who sent Christ, draws us to Himself (John 6:44). The greatest story ever told is found in Isaiah 9:6-7a. It's a story about a Child who is born, a Son who is given, and the fact that the government will be on His shoulder, and His precious name will be called Wonderful, Counselor, Mighty God, Everlasting Father and Prince of Peace. That's not all; of the increase of His government and peace there will be no end.

Christ is the hero that swoops in and saves us when we accept Him as Lord and Savior and begin a new life in Him. He rescues us out of the hand of the villain. He has won the battle for us. We really get to live happily ever after in our own story, once we accept Jesus Christ as our Lord and Savior.

Do you know Him? Are you a triumphant victor in the greatest story ever told? Has the enemy of your soul been defeated (1 Peter 5:8)? Are you living happily ever after today because you are saved? Will you live happily ever after in the ages to come?

Time to Reflect

Scripture: Isaiah 9:6-7a

Observation: What are some of your thoughts and feelings after reflecting on Christ?

Application: What can you start, stop or continue doing? How is your life story, since you accepted Jesus Christ as your Savior?

Prayer: If you have not accepted Jesus as your Lord and Savior or you need to rededicate your life to Jesus, refer to pages xviii-xix; review those scriptures and pray the Prayer of Repentance. Tell others about your newfound faith in Christ Jesus. Seek out a Bible-teaching church. Join that congregation and begin your journey in the greatest story ever told.

If you are saved, pray about any <u>one</u> of the suggested options below. You are not expected to do all three unless the Holy Spirit directs you otherwise.

What can you commit to Jesus?
What do you want Him to do for you?
What do you want Him to help you to do?

Deeper Still: Using a good study Bible with commentary, review the following Scriptures concerning the story of Christ and us: *John 3:1-21; Eph. 2:1-10; Rom.8:28-29.*

Praise and Worship: What praise or worship song comes to mind as you conclude our devotional for the day? I encourage you to listen to it now. Below is my playlist, which has a variety of artists and genres, so hold on and enjoy it if you care to partake.

"Bread of Heaven" – Fred Hammond – [lyrics][6]
"In Christ Alone" – Shane & Shane[7]

---

[6] Fred Hammond, "Bread of Heaven [lyrics]," uploaded by ChristianFellowship5, August 26, 2009, YouTube music video, 5:01, https://www.youtube.com/watch?v=kjVgm9-XTqQ.

[7] Shane & Shane, "In Christ Alone," provided by Catapult Reservatory, LLC, August 28, 2018, YouTube music video, 4:36, https://www.youtube.com/watch?v=aLOsM3ON-24.

THE TRUEST STORY EVER TOLD

John 17:17, 1:1, 18:37

In our postmodern world, truth has lost its meaning. Truth has become something that is only in the eye of the beholder. Truth is declared as something that is relative only to the person making the truth claim. In fact, if you ask those around you what truth is (try it as an experiment today), you might hear things like: *It's whatever you want it to be … That is your truth, but not my truth … Well, that is true for you, but not true for me … How can we really know truth?* And the list could go on.

What does it mean when we say something is true? I heard Josh McDowell, author of *Evidence that Demands a Verdict*, describe truth this way, "Truth is that which has fidelity to the original. Something that is the same as or equal to the original." (McDowell, 2017) When I heard this, I got it. It made a lot of sense.

In the world of Apologetics, there is what is known as the theory of correspondence. This means what you say is true should actually correspond to what is occurring. For example, if I say it is 90 degrees outside and I am in Chicago in January, there is a high degree of likelihood that this would not correspond to what is actually happening with the weather outside. When Jesus said, "…He was born to bear witness to the truth and everyone who hears His voice is of the truth" (John 18:37), we can see a twofold correspondence occurring. Let's examine the first corresponding truth. Jesus said, "He was born to bear witness to the truth." What is that truth? That He is the Savior of the world (John 3:16), that He came to seek and to save that which was lost (Luke 19:10) and that we would have life more abundantly (John 10:10b). The second corresponding truth is that His sheep know His voice (John 10:4-5, 5:25).

The believer in Christ will have none of this postmodern nonsense. He or she knows that truth is found in Jesus Christ, the Son of the living God (Matthew 16:16).

Time to Reflect

Scripture: John 17:17, 1:1, 18:37

Observation: What are some of your thoughts and feelings after reflecting on the truth about Christ?

Application: What can you start, stop or continue doing?

Prayer: Pray about any <u>one</u> of the suggested options below. You are not expected to do all three unless the Holy Spirit directs you otherwise.

What can you commit to Jesus?
What do you want Him to do for you?
What do you want Him to help you to do?

Deeper Still: Using a good study Bible with commentary, review the following Scriptures concerning Jesus and truth: *John 1:14, 14:6*. Also, review these Scriptures concerning God and truth: *Deut. 32:4; 2 Sam. 7:28; Ps. 33:4, 115:1, 146:6; Isa. 65:16; Rom. 3:4.*

Praise and Worship: What praise or worship song comes to mind as you conclude our devotional for the day? I encourage you to listen to it now. Below is my playlist, which has a variety of artists and genres, so hold on and enjoy it if you care to partake.

"Jesus Is" – Brooklyn Tabernacle Choir – (Lyrics)[8]
"His Truth Is Marching On – Wintley Phipps – pay close attention to verse two[9]

---

[8] Brooklyn Tabernacle Choir, "Jesus Is Lyrics," uploaded by Lyrics Videos, February 19, 2018, YouTube music video, 4:23, https://www.youtube.com/watch?v=mWWNiNJ1Utk.

[9] Wintley Phipps, "His Truth Is Marching On," provided by Catapult Reservatory, LLC. April 2, 2020. YouTube music video, 4:27 https://www.youtube.com/watch?v=cSK28dD2Y9E.

JESUS AND THE FATHER ARE ONE

John 10:30

Jesus was not just some good man, as some believe. Nor was He just a good teacher with good moral attributes. Jesus and the Father are one. This does not mean that God the Father and God the Son are equivalent like a child's transformer toy that morphs into a different figure when you twist it in a few easy directions.

When Jesus says He and His Father are one, He is saying that He and the Father have unity of nature and essence. In other words, they are both God. Now this gets us into the trinity. The word trinity is not found in the Bible, but the concept is clearly established in the Word of God (Matt. 28:19; John 14:26; 15:26; 2 Cor. 13:14; 1 Peter 1:2; 1 John 5:7).

The trinity is a very challenging doctrine in Scripture, but it is clearly evident. The best way that I know to understand the trinity is to establish some basic facts.

- We do not believe in three separate gods, which is tritheism. The Bible does not teach this about God. The Bible clearly states that the Lord God is one (Deuteronomy 6:4).

- The Father is not the Son and the Father is not the Holy Spirit.

- The Son is not the Father and the Son is not the Holy Spirit.

- The Holy Spirit is not the Father and the Holy Spirit is not the Son.

- The Father is God, the Son is God and the Holy Spirit is God.

- The one true God is co-equal, co-eternal, co-essence. In other words, there is unity of nature and essence (John 5:17-23; 17:22).

Time to Reflect

Scripture: John 10:30

Observation: What are some of your thoughts and feelings after reflecting on the fact that Jesus and God are one?

Application: How does this knowledge help you to understand Jesus?

Prayer: Pray about any <u>one</u> of the suggested options below. You are not expected to do all three unless the Holy Spirit directs you otherwise.

What can you commit to Jesus?
What do you want Him to do for you?
What do you want Him to help you to do?

Deeper Still: Using a good study Bible with commentary, review the following Scriptures concerning Jesus' oneness with the Father: *Mark 9:37; John 1:18; 5:19; 5:30; 6:57; 8:16; 8:29; 10:38; 12:45; 14:7; 14:10; 14:20; 15:23; 16:15; 17:10-11; 17:21-22; Acts 10:38; 1 Cor. 3:23; 2 Cor. 5:19; Phil. 2:6; 2 John 1:9.*

Praise and Worship: What praise or worship song comes to mind as you conclude our devotional for the day? I encourage you to listen to it now. Below is my playlist, which has a variety of artists and genres, so hold on and enjoy it if you care to partake.

"Holy, Holy, Holy" – Joseph Larson – It's My Desire DVD[10]
"Come Thou Almighty King" – (Live from Sing! '21)–Keith & Kristyn Getty, Tommy Bailey[11]
"Trinity Hymn" – Mak Jeschke – (Lyric Video)[12]
"We Believe Apostle's Creed"–Keith & Kristyn Getty – Lyric[13]

---

[10] Joseph Larson, "Holy, Holy, Holy," provided by TuneCore, May 19, 2015, YouTube music video, 7:55, https://www.youtube.com/watch?v=cpNuIfUCVZc.

[11] Keith & Kristyn Getty, "Come Thou Almighty King (Live from Sing! '21)," uploaded by Keith and Kristyn Getty, April 19, 2022, YouTube music video, 3:31, https://www.youtube.com/watch?v=NT4IvKk8Yko.

[12] Mark Jeshke, "Trinity Hymn (Lyric Video)," provided by Mark Jeschke, April 20, 2022, YouTube music video, 5:11, https://www.youtube.com/watch?v=MbOG8oN2G8E.

[13] Keith & Kristyn Getty, "We Believe Apostle's Creed Lyric," uploaded by Trinity Fellowship, January 16, 2017, YouTube music video, 4:50, https://www.youtube.com/watch?v=vZqX13gEbCM.

JESUS: THE VERY BRIGHTNESS OF HIS GLORY

Hebrews 1:3

When I look across the water beyond my deck, the rays of the sun are reflected as they dance across the pond. They are so bright that I must shield my eyes in order to take in the light and beauty. The brilliance of the rays is more than I can take in with the naked eye, it is radiant. Radiance is an overwhelming, intense light or brilliance coming from that, which is glorious beyond words.

As we reflect on our Scripture today, Hebrews 1:3 has some of the most profound words about the image of Jesus, the Son of God, in Scripture. I wonder if you caught it when you read it. "Who being the brightness of His glory..." Now take a moment to just think about what is being said here and let it really soak into your spirit. Jesus is the brightness and light, the radiance of His (God the Father's) glory. While many commentaries will say that Jesus reflected the glory of the Father, according to MacArthur[14], "the Son is not just reflecting His Father's glory, He is God and radiates His own essential glory." The notes of the New King James Version Study Bible say, "This is an inherent brightness like a ray from the sun. Jesus' glorious brightness comes from being essentially divine" (Earl D. Radmacher, 2007).

Jesus' perfection, attributes, character and morality are an expression of His and the Father's brightness, radiance, light and glory. Jesus, the second person in the trinity is more than a mere man, the good Lord or the man upstairs, as some unwittingly characterize Him. He is the very radiance. He is God!

---

[14] MacArthur NKJV, (MacArthur, 1997), commentary notes Hebrew 1:3

Scripture: Hebrews 1:3

Observation: What are some of your thoughts and feelings after reflecting on the fact that Jesus radiates His own essential glory as God?

Application: How does this knowledge help you to understand Jesus as God?

Prayer: Pray about any <u>one</u> of the suggested options below. You are not expected to do all three unless the Holy Spirit directs you otherwise.

What can you commit to Jesus?
What do you want Him to do for you?
What do you want Him to help you to do?

Deeper Still: Using a good study Bible with commentary, review the following scriptures concerning Jesus' radiance: *John 1:4-5, 14; 8:12; 2 Cor. 4:4, 6.*

Praise and Worship: What praise or worship song comes to mind as you conclude our devotional for the day? I encourage you to listen to it now. Below is my playlist, which has a variety of artists and genres, so hold on and enjoy it if you care to partake.

"Oh the Glory of Your Presence" – Ron Kenoly – Live[15] 15
"Jesus, You're Beautiful – CeCe Winans – Official Audio[16] 16
"Walk in the Light" – Posted by Charles Pope[17] 17

---

[15] Ron Kenoly, "Oh the Glory of Your Presence [Live], provided by Absolute Marketing International Ltd, June 23, 2015, YouTube music video, 4:37, https://www.youtube.com/watch?v=F4TYwm4aQ4U.

[16] CeCe Winans, "Jesus, You're Beautiful (Official Audio)," uploaded by CeCe Winans, March 12, 2021, YouTube music video, 7:13, https://www.youtube.com/watch?v=daWu1MBbx5M.

[17] "Walk in the Light," uploaded by Charles Pope, April 2, 2011, YouTube music video, 5:42, https://www.youtube.com/watch?v=GCTR0WXZjwk.

INTERNAL BIBLICAL EVIDENCE FOR JESUS AS THE CHRIST

John 14:1-6

Some believe that Jesus' last name was Christ. This is not true. The term Christ is the Greek title (Cristos) and the Hebrew title Messiah (Mashiah), which both mean anointed one.

When one refers to the internal, biblical evidence for the Christ, we are asking, *What evidence does the Bible give for Jesus as the Christ? How do we know He is the way? Couldn't He just be a mere angel, man or a deity among other gods?* The internal evidence of scriptures will have none of this nonsense. The Old Testament prophetically declares that a deliverer would come to save His people (Isaiah 7:14; Is. 61:1-2; Matthew 1:21). Jesus was that deliverer. He fulfilled prophecy (Luke 24:27, 44; Acts 10:43; 18:28).

Lee Strobel, in *The Case for Christ*, examines in depth the internal, biblical evidence that points to Him being the Christ. Strobel refers to this evidence as the fingerprint evidence, which clearly describes that Jesus fulfilled prophecy with amazing accuracy. There is too much fingerprint evidence of the fulfillment of the many Old Testament Scriptures pointing to the Christ to ascribe Jesus' life as a mere coincidence (Strobel, 2016). He is the Christ, the Anointed One, the Holy One of Israel and the Savior of the world (Matthew 16:13-16; Mark 1:24).

Let's compare and contrast John the Baptist and Jesus. The priests and Levites saw something unique in John the Baptist. In John 1:19-20, they questioned John as to who he was and he plainly declared that he was not the Christ. Jesus confirmed, on the other hand, that He was as they said (the Christ). He is the anointed one. He was sent from God and He is God. The religious leaders had the Romans to crucify Him for the very charge of blasphemy because He made Himself equal with God (Matthew 26:63- 66). The scriptural evidence is quite clear.

Finally, when He was in the upper room giving His disciples final instructions in John 14:1-6, Thomas seemed a bit confused and wanted to know how they could know the way. Jesus declared that He is the way to the Father. Our Scripture today emphatically declares that He is the one and only way, the truth and the life. "No one comes to the Father except through Me." Jesus the Christ is the anointed one prophesied about in the Old Testament. The evidence is overwhelming within the Scriptures that He is exactly whom He says He is, the exclusive Christ, the Anointed One, prophesied about in the Old Testament, who has come. All roads don't lead to God the Father. There is only one way and it is narrow (Matthew 7:14). Only through Jesus Christ and no other is one saved and the biblical evidence of this fact is overwhelming (John 8:24; Acts 4:12)!

Time to Reflect

Scripture: John 14:1-6

Observation: What are some of your thoughts and feelings after reflecting on the fact that Jesus is the one and only Anointed One?

Application: How does this knowledge help you to appreciate Jesus?

Prayer: Pray about any <u>one</u> of the suggested options below. You are not expected to do all three unless the Holy Spirit directs you otherwise.

What can you commit to Jesus?
What do you want Him to do for you?
What do you want Him to help you to do?

Deeper Still: Using a good study Bible with commentary, review the following Scriptures concerning Jesus as the Christ: *John 1:14; 3:15; 6:68; 11:25; Matt. 7:13-14; Luke 13:24*; 1 Cor. 2:2; 3:11).

Praise and Worship: What praise or worship song comes to mind as you conclude our devotional for the day? I encourage you to listen to it now. Below is my playlist, which has a variety of artists and genres, so hold on and enjoy it if you care to partake.

"The Way" – Pat Barrett – New Horizon – Lyric Video[18]
"Maranatha Singers–Thy Word [with lyrics]"[19]

---

[18] Pat Barrett, "The Way (New Horizon) (Lyric Video)," April 13, 2018, YouTube music video, 4:19, https://www.youtube.com/watch?v=MOzsJlk8p6I.

[19] Maranatha! Music, "Maranatha Singers - Thy Word [with lyrics]," uploaded by Worship Videos, August 24, 2015, YouTube music video, 3:33, https://www.youtube.com/watch?v=npWJZwgmKMo

EXTERNAL EVIDENCE FOR JESUS AS THE CHRIST

John 20:30-31, 21:25

It's one thing for the Bible to proclaim that Jesus is the Christ, the Messiah, the Anointed One, the Holy One of Israel sent by the Father. It's another thing to possess forensic evidence outside of the Bible (external evidence), which verifies and corresponds with the truth of the internal (inside the Bible) evidence. You may wonder if such evidence actually exists.

As in a court of law, we must present and examine the external evidence to determine if our biblical claims are supported by anything other than what the Bible says. For us as believers, it's enough for us to hang our hat on Scripture alone. But for the skeptic who argues from points outside of Scripture, the question is, "Do we have any supporting documentation from non-biblical sources that substantiates the Christian claim about Jesus as the Christ?"

Ah, here is where "The Case for Christ" by Lee Strobel enters the picture. Lee, a onetime atheist (who we mentioned yesterday) set out to reexamine the case for Christ. He launched an all-out investigation into the facts surrounding the case for Christianity. Lee's experience as a legal affairs editor of the *Chicago Tribune*, coupled with his Yale Law Degree, led him through a journey which highlighted overwhelming evidence for Christianity and the case for Christ. (Strobel, *The Case for Christ Study Guide*, 2013)

Strobel expertly compares how one would examine in a court of law all of the facts to determine if there is enough evidence to convict the claims of Christianity. In his bestselling book, he examines the eyewitness evidence, documentary evidence, corroborating evidence, scientific evidence, rebuttal evidence, identity evidence, psychological evidence, medical evidence, and the missing body evidence. It is a fascinating read that helps us to understand and validate the historical, archeological, and scientific claims for Jesus as the Christ. The short of it is this: there is an overwhelming abundance of evidence to charge the biblical narrative with guilt. What the Bible claims is true can be supported by outside evidence.[20] [21]

---

[20] Lee Strobel, "The Case for Christ," uploaded by Passion City Church, July 1, 2018, YouTube conference video, 39:52, https://www.youtube.com/watch?v=67uj2qvQi_k.

[21] Lee Strobel, "The Case for Christ Documentary," uploaded by ChannelC2, November 13, 2021, YouTube video, 1:11:26, https://www.youtube.com/results?search_query=the+case+for+christ+lee+strobel+documentary.

Time to Reflect

Scripture: John 20:30-31; 21:25

Observation: What are some of your thoughts and feelings after hearing or reading some of the external evidence that validates Jesus as the Christ?

Application: How does this knowledge help you to understand Jesus?

Prayer: Pray about any <u>one</u> of the suggested options below. You are not expected to do all three unless the Holy Spirit directs you otherwise.

What can you commit to Jesus?
What do you want Him to do for you?
What do you want Him to help you to do?

Deeper Still: Using a good study Bible with commentary, review the following Scriptures concerning Jesus as the Christ: *John 14:26; 16:13-15.*

Praise and Worship: What praise or worship song comes to mind as you conclude our devotional for the day? I encourage you to listen to it now. Below is my playlist, which has a variety of artists and genres, so hold on and enjoy it if you care to partake.

"Lord, I Lift Your Name on High" – Maranatha! Music – Lyric Video[22]
"Real" – Pastor Fleetwood Irving[23]

---

[22] Maranatha! Music, "Lord I Lift Your Name on High (Lyric Video)," uploaded by Maranatha! Music, March 30, 2016, YouTube music video, 4:23, https://www.youtube.com/watch?v=tQiapzfQoq0.

[23] Fleetwood Irving, "Real (Jesus is Real to Me)," uploaded by Deborrah Ogans, January 22, 2012, YouTube music video, 3:01, https://www.youtube.com/watch?v=RzKxBHwPE_s.

Week 2: Why is Christ Important?

"Love comes in the
shape of a cross."
~ Dr. Tony Evans

YOUR CREDENTIALS OR WORKS
WILL NOT QUALIFY YOU FOR HEAVEN

Romans 3:10-12

I used to teach World Religions and my curriculum separated all religions into two types. One type is monotheistic. Monotheistic religions have followers who believe in a transcendent God[24]. This type of religion includes Christianity, Judaism and Islam. On the opposite end of the spectrum are eastern and native religions whose focus is on the internal energy or some type of mysterious external power(s). Within Evangelical circles, I have heard that all religions can be divided in two ways: religion is either based on 1) faith (Christianity) or 2) works (all other religions) for salvation or ultimate fulfillment.

The Bible teaches that works won't save us. Man needs a Savior who is Jesus Christ. In Philippians 3:3-10, Paul gives a biography of his Jewish credentials and works. After listing them for the Judaizers,[25] he concludes and declares all of his credentials are rubbish. The King James Version uses the word dung. You get the point. Paul knew that his pedigree, accomplishments and past behavior would not give him eternal life. Paul recognized that grace through faith in Jesus was the only way for man to be reconciled to the Father (Ephesians 2:8-10). He didn't confuse his accomplishments or works by comparing himself to other men (2 Corinthians 10:12, 17). He knew that the life that he now lived had to be lived by faith in the Son of God (Galatians 2:20).

There are six soul-searching questions you should ask yourself today. The answers to these questions will highlight the importance of Christ in your life and you must answer each question correctly. (Ninety-nine and a half won't do):

1)   Am I secretly relying on my credentials and works to get me into heaven?

2)   Is my belief in Christ based on grace and faith alone, or am I relying on my works and achievements to give me eternal life?

3)   Am I committed to becoming a disciple of Christ?

4)   Does my heart hunger and thirst for His righteousness? (Matthew 5:6)

5)   Do I compare myself with others and think, "I am not as bad as she or he is?"

6)   What is my heart really like? (Jeremiah 17:9)

---

[24] Transcendent God: A God who is separate and even somewhat remote from nature, history, and humanity. (Erickson M.)

[25] Judaizers: People who attempted to impose the standards and laws of Judaism upon Christianity. Some of the early Christians, for example, would have required Gentile converts to be circumcised and keep the Mosaic Law. (Erickson M.)

Time to Reflect

Scripture: Romans 3:10-12

Observation: What are some of your thoughts and feelings after considering whether you are relying on faith in Jesus or your credentials to get you into heaven?

Application: How does this knowledge help you to understand Jesus?

Prayer: Pray about any <u>one</u> of the suggested options below. You are not expected to do all three unless the Holy Spirit directs you otherwise.

What can you commit to Jesus?
What do you want Him to do for you?
What do you want Him to help you to do?

Deeper Still: Using a good study Bible with commentary, review the following Scriptures concerning the insufficiency of our credentials and works to qualify for heaven: *Isa. 57:12; Ezek. 18:24; Matt. 7:22-23; Rom. 3:20; 9:32; 11:6; Gal. 2:16; 2 Tim. 1:9; Titus 3:4-5.*

Praise and Worship: What praise or worship song comes to mind as you conclude our devotional for the day? I encourage you to listen to it now. Below is my playlist, which has a variety of artists and genres, so hold on and enjoy it if you care to partake.

"No Other Name" – Don Moen[26]
"It's My Desire" – Joseph Larson[27]

---

[26] Don Moen, "No Other Name," uploaded by The Watchers Worship, January 21, 2016, YouTube music video, 4:12, https://www.youtube.com/watch?v=z40TLeD3_mo.

[27] Joseph Larson, "It's My Desire (Live)," provided to YouTube by TuneCore, May 19, 2015, YouTube music video, 6:45, https://www.youtube.com/watch?v=halzlop2hps.

⊙NLY JESUS CAN RECONCILE

2 Corinthians 5:15-21

Relationships become broken in life. Something happens and a psychological wound can tear the best of friends apart. Some won't come back together for years. Sadly, some never mend and the comrades live and die separately when only years earlier they were bosom buddies. I remember my best friend of 34 years told me during a painful period in our relationship that she did not want to reconcile and she would just see me in heaven. I am so glad the two of us stuck it out and worked through our differences. She has gone to be with the Lord now, but I was able to be by her side and praise God with her as she transitioned to glory. Mending relationships is so important. So much so that God the Father did just that for us.

Theologically, the doctrine of reconciliation teaches the bringing together of God with man through the finished work of Jesus Christ on the cross.

When Adam and Eve sinned in the garden, they plunged all of humanity into a broken and disconnected state with God our creator. There was only one way that man could be reconciled with God. There needed to be a perfect sacrifice that would satisfy God the Father (Romans 3:24-25). Jesus, the Christ, was the perfect sacrifice. He alone could reconcile man to God (2 Corinthians 5:18). There was no other way back to the Father. We learned yesterday that our works and credentials will not help us obtain eternal life with God the Father in any way.

As I write this, I think of my family members, coworkers and neighbors who are good, nice people. They do great works and don't bother anyone. But, they are not reconciled in Christ. They don't know Him. They don't understand the good news, that Jesus reconciles us and is the satisfying sacrifice that enables us to have eternal life.

As our Pastor teaches us, we are called to win the lost around us. We must begin with those with whom we have a relationship, those closest to us. We must tell them about Jesus and give them the good news that only Jesus can reconcile man to the Father. If Christ is important to us, we have an obligation to others to convey His importance as our reconciler with passion, compassion and love.

Time to Reflect

Scripture: 2 Corinthians 5:15-21

Observation: What are some of your thoughts about Christ as the one who reconciles us?

Application: How does this knowledge help you to love Jesus more?

Prayer: Pray about any <u>one</u> of the suggested options below. You are not expected to do all three unless the Holy Spirit directs you otherwise.

What can you commit to Jesus?
What do you want Him to do for you?
What do you want Him to help you to do?

Deeper Still: Using a good study Bible with commentary, review the following Scriptures concerning Jesus as He who reconciles us with the Father: *Eph. 2:16; Col. 1:20; Heb. 2:17.*

Praise and Worship: What praise or worship song comes to mind as you conclude our devotional for the day? I encourage you to listen to it now. Below is my playlist, which has a variety of artists and genres, so hold on and enjoy it if you care to partake.

"Jesus Is The Answer" – Andrae Crouch[28]
"Please Forgive Me [Live]"–Gaither Vocal Band–Michael English[29]
"God So Loved ft. We the Kingdom (Live)" – Tasha Cobbs Leonard – ft. We the Kingdom (Live)[30]
"Is He Worthy" – Keith & Kristyn Getty[31]

---

[28] Andrae Crouch, "Jesus is the Answer," uploaded by Walter Robinson Jr., January 13, 2015, YouTube music video, 4:59, https://www.youtube.com/watch?v=cKHpweGR7Bs.

[29] Gaither Vocal Band, Michael English, "Please Forgive Me [Live]," uploaded by Gaither Music TV, August 16, 2012, YouTube music video, 5:07, https://www.youtube.com/watch?v=aGW1x_ILp2o.

[30] Tasha Cobbs Leonard, "God So Loved ft. We the Kingdom (Live) ft. We the Kingdom," uploaded by Tasha Cobbs Leonard, October 23, 2020, YouTube music video, 7:07, https://www.youtube.com/watch?v=iVux5s-SWFc

[31] Keith & Kristyn Getty Ft. Chris Tomlin, "Is He Worthy? (Live from Sing! '21)," uploaded by Keith and Kristyn Getty, April 8, 2022, YouTube music video, 4:37, https://www.youtube.com/watch?v=As77j073jxM.

THE CROSS OF CHRIST MAKES THE DIFFERENCE

Hebrews 9:22

You have heard it said before: "That right there really doesn't matter in the larger picture;" meaning, that thing can be dismissed or thought of as trite. However, the cross of Jesus Christ is not one to be thought of as an inconsequential, light thing. It was at the cross where our sins were forgiven. Without the cross, there is no remission of sins. Remission is a theological term that means forgiveness. The shed blood reconciled the relationship between God and the sinner. The blood atones and makes amends for our sins because there is life in the blood (Leviticus 17:11).

So let's examine today why this cross is so important. The cross cost God something. It cost him the sacrifice of His one and only Son (John 3:16). The cross separated the Son from the Father (Matthew 27:46), a pain and an anguish never experienced by the Son. And, He did this all for you and me, so that we might have life and have it more abundantly (John 10:10). The cross makes the true believer long for this Savior that would pay it all on Calvary. The sacrifice of Christ causes us to cry out like Paul and say, "that I may know Him..." (Philippians 3:10). The cross causes me to conform to the image of God (Romans 12:2).

I am encouraged by these seven reasons for the importance of the cross: (Thompson, p. 1726; Chain Ref. No. 892)

1.   The cross is important because it has a doctrine (1 Cor. 1:17; 2:2; Gal. 5:11; Col. 1:20).

2.   The cross is important because of its message (1 Corinthians 1:17).

3.   The cross is important because of its glory (Galatians 6:14).

4.   The cross is important because of its reconciliation (Ephesians 2:16).

5.   The cross is important because of its enemies (Philippians 3:18).

6.   The cross is important because of its peace (Colossians 1:20).

7.   The cross is important because of its accomplishment (Colossians 2:14).

Scripture: Hebrews 9:22

Observation: What are some of your thoughts about the cross and what it accomplished for you?

Application: How does this knowledge help you to love Christ more?

Prayer: Pray about any <u>one</u> of the suggested options below. You are not expected to do all three unless the Holy Spirit directs you otherwise.

What can you commit to Jesus?
What do you want Him to do for you?
What do you want Him to help you to do?

Deeper Still: Using a good study Bible with commentary, review the following Scriptures concerning the cross of Christ: *Gal. 6:14; Heb. 12:2.*

Praise and Worship: What praise or worship song comes to mind as you conclude our devotional for the day? I encourage you to listen to it now. Below is my playlist, which has a variety of artists and genres, so hold on and enjoy it if you care to partake.

"The Blood/Because He Lives" – CeCe Winans[32]
"Cross Made the Difference" – Adam Crabb[33]
"Old Rugged Cross" – Rev. Frankie Coleman[34]
"Oh The Blood Medley" – FWC Resurrection Choir[35]
"I Know That Jesus Loves Me" – Vanessa Burge Garner[36]

---

[32] CeCe Winans, "The Blood/Because He Lives," uploaded by Marquis Robertson, April 14, 2020, YouTube music video, 4:30, https://www.youtube.com/watch?v=ZwByK7XPwHl.

[33] Adam Crabb, "Cross Made the Difference," provided by Daywind Records, May 16, 2019, YouTube music video, 5:05, https://www.youtube.com/watch?v=xDRFP1xBkf4.

[34] Frankie Coleman, "The Old Rugged Cross," provided by CDBaby, November 5, 2015, YouTube music video, 11:09, https://www.youtube.com/watch?v=5wdfClYmapo.

[35] FWC Resurrection Choir, "Oh the Blood Medley (FWC Resurrection Choir)," uploaded by Hayden Mccallum, February 13, 2023, YouTube music video, 7:03, https://www.youtube.com/watch?v=_-IG7rNhGcA.

[36] Vanessa Burge Garner, "I Know That Jesus Loves Me," provided by CDBaby, June 22, 2017, YouTube music video, 4:16, https://www.youtube.com/watch?v=P8WR6vJEAx4.

SEPARATION AT BIRTH –
ABANDONING THE GIFT OF FERTILE SOIL

Judges 13

The last time I studied the life of Samson, I discovered something I had not considered in the many years I have been reading his story. Please allow me to use an analogy of soil to compare the roots of the family into which one is born. I am proposing that every family has either fertile or unfertile soil for God to grow in a child's life. With this said, let's examine the abandonment of the gift of fertile soil from birth.

One can imagine that Samson abandoned the fertile soil of his birth narrative by abandoning his upbringing. Let me explain a bit more. He was born to two faithful parents who followed God. He was set apart from birth to be a Nazirite, yet he turned his back throughout his life on this fertile soil in which he was to grow and become cultivated for God's use and purpose. Bent on doing his own thing and achieving his own destiny, his life actually went (by his doings) into a progressive abandonment of his God-given Nazirite separation.

Look closely. Samson is born at a time when the Philistines are oppressing his people. The announcement of his birth is accompanied by what theologians describe as a theophany, which is an appearance of God Himself in the Old Testament. He is born to a mother who was barren before receiving a special visitation from God. Sampson is a miracle promised son to this infertile couple (Judges 13:3.) Samson's mother is given specific instructions as to how she is to proceed with her pregnancy (Judges 13:4, 7) and what his unique position will be within the Jewish community. All of this is happening before he is even born. Samson's Nazirite separation means he is to be consecrated; and the rules that he has to follow are: no wine, shaving, defilement, or corruption (Numbers 6:3-8). Despite being born into a Godly family and being raised according to this God-given consecration, fertile soil is squandered by the choices Samson makes.

Let's fast forward and follow his irresponsible separation from God. Samson's professional life as a judge only gets a passing mention in Scripture, but his private life is a mess. In fact, when I last taught his story, I entitled Judges 13-16 "The Messiness of Sin and the Providence of God." If you follow his story through Judges chapters 14-16, you find that he increasingly abandons his godly separation. He is downright reckless in his pursuit of things that are antithetical to his consecration at birth. He comes in contact with dead bodies (Judges 14:6, 8), he marries a Philistine (Judges 14:2-3), his wife is murdered because of him (Judges 15:6), he takes revenge on the Philistines (Judges 15:7), he hooks up with Delilah (not his wife) (Judges 16:4) and he ends his life by committing suicide and taking revenge (Judges 16:28). While he is credited with slaying more Philistines at his death than while he lived, Samson's life is a tragic story of impulsive, ungodly behavior by one who should have known better (Judges 16:30).

While your birth may not have been as spectacular as Samson's, the roots of godly seeds may have been planted at an early age as the fertile soil for your life. Even if this is not your story, God still has called you to be His and He has a particular way in which He expects you and me to grow and mature in Him. Because we are in Christ, Paul says in 2 Corinthians 6:17 that we are to be separate and not touch what is unclean. When Christ is important in our lives. we will progressively cultivate the fertile God- given soil for our lives. We will not progressively abandon our separation for our own foolish whims and desires, but we will separate and consecrate our lives humbly and gratefully to Him.

Have you abandoned the gift of Christ's fertile soil in your life in order to do your own thing? How important is Christ to you?

Scripture: Judges 13

Observation: What are some of your thoughts about Samson and him abandoning his separation from birth?

Application: How does this knowledge help you to follow Paul's encouragement to the Corinthians to be separate?

Prayer: Pray about any <u>one</u> of the suggested options below. You are not expected to do all three unless the Holy Spirit directs you otherwise.

What can you commit to Jesus?
What do you want Him to do for you?
What do you want Him to help you to do?

Deeper Still: Using a good Study Bible with commentary, review the following Scriptures concerning the believer's separate life, which is to be lived in Christ: *1 Cor. 6:11-20; 1 Cor. 10:20-21; 2 Cor. 6:11-18; Eph. 4:24; 5:11.*

Praise and Worship: What praise or worship song comes to mind as you conclude our devotional for the day? I encourage you to listen to it now. Below is my playlist, which has a variety of artists and genres, so hold on and enjoy it if you care to partake.

"You Are My All In All/Canon in D (Live)" – David Phelps[37]
"What Can Separate You?" – Babbie Mason[38]
"I Will Run to You" – Alvin Slaughter[39]

---

[37] David Phelps, "You Are My All In All/Canon in D (Live)," uploaded by Gaither Music TV, November 22, 2012, YouTube music video, 5:13, https://www.youtube.com/watch?v=OLilYpRAuU4.

[38] Babbie Mason, "What Can Separate you?" uploaded by Al Bums, April 18, 2017, YouTube music video, 4:42, https://www.youtube.com/watch?v=PMCn3HEIAX0.

[39] Alvin Slaughter, "I Will Run to You," uploaded by awayclouds, July 27, 2009, YouTube music video, 9:50, https://www.youtube.com/watch?v=jnfy9NcjAkU.

THERE ARE CONSEQUENCES FOR UNBELIEF

John 3:18, 36

If you ask most churchgoers, they will confess a belief in Christ. Yet they are religious, but not converted. The perversion of this fact is that we don't even know the enemy is deceiving us. The Pharisees can serve as a big, bright, shiny mirror for every confessing churchgoer. John 5:39-47 is a passage that serves as a scathing warning to us all. The consequences of unbelief are punishment and death (Rom. 6:23; Heb. 10:29)

These super-religious people, missed the whole point of Jesus' life, miracles and signs - which were all done to authenticate that He was the Son of God. They trusted in Moses who was only a shadow of the true deliverer who was to come. If we are not careful, we will place our salvation and confidence in shadows of our own fake fruit, thinking we are experiencing the real deal. Any time our primary focus is in a church, a pastor or works that are more about personal growth and recognition, and less about the fact we have been with Jesus, a warning light should go off for us. Paul says in 2 Corinthians 13:5 that we are to examine ourselves to discern whether or not we are in the faith. John 3:20 illustrates the actions of an unbeliever. 2 John 1:9 teaches that a true believer abides in the doctrine of Christ.

What are some ways we can check our salvation? James 2:21-26 illustrates that our faith will be completed with works. John 3:21 tells us that we will know the truth and it will come to the light for our deeds to be clearly seen. 1 John 5:3 lets us know that His commandments are not burdensome.

I know I am saved, but it is good to constantly evaluate my salvation and walk in the mirror of God's Word. When we come to the conclusion that there is nothing we can do to obtain a right standing in God and that it is all about what Christ did to obtain that righteousness for us, we are in right standing and good works are an outflow.

I don't know about you, but I don't want to trick myself into believing I am saved when I am not. John 2:25 tells me that He knows exactly what is in me. This is why Ephesians 2:8-10 says that salvation is by grace through faith. Christ is too important to succumb to a deceitful heart. Is He really your Lord?

Scripture: John 3:18, 36

Observation: What are some of your thoughts about unbelief and a deceitful heart?

Application: How does this knowledge help you to commit more deeply to being a true disciple of Christ?

Prayer: Pray about any <u>one</u> of the suggested options below. You are not expected to do all three unless the Holy Spirit directs you otherwise.

What can you commit to Jesus
What do you want Him to do for you?
What do you want Him to help you to do?

Deeper Still: Using a good study Bible with commentary, study each element for fruitful growth in Christ as found in *2 Peter 1:5-10*.

Praise and Worship: What praise or worship song comes to mind as you conclude our devotional for the day? I encourage you to listen to it now. Below is my playlist, which has a variety of artists and genres, so hold on and enjoy it if you care to partake.

"He Knows My Name" – Maranatha Singers[40]
"Come Thou Fount (I Will Sing)" – Chris Tomlin[41]
"I Believe" – Jonathan Nelson[42]

---

[40] Maranatha Singers, "He Knows My Name," uploaded Julz P, March 16, 2007, YouTube music video, 3:25, https://www.youtube.com/watch?v=hXsiWoyjw60.

[41] Chris Tomlin, "Come Thou Fount (I Will Sing)," provided by Universal Music Group, July 24, 2018, YouTube music video, 4:59, https://www.youtube.com/watch?v=9OIusL_X8Jw.

[42] Jonathan Nelson, "I Believe (Island Medley) (So Long Bye Bye) (Radio Edit)," provided by Entertainment One Distribution US, May 1, 2016, YouTube music video, 4:00, https://www.youtube.com/watch?v=LUCN0G5dtf0.

HE SAYS, "FOLLOW ME"

Luke 9:23-26, John 12:26

This week we have been examining why Christ is important. We established in week one that He is the Son of God. This week, we are examining reasons why He is important in the believer's life.

The command to "Follow Me" is a primary call for the believer. It is a personal and relational call from the Savior. Salvation is coupled with a radical devotion and commitment to want to follow Him and to do His will. The Holy Spirit plants this in the life of true believers. Believers who follow Christ are not caught up in doing their own thing and fitting Him into their schedule. True believers who are willing to deny themselves, not procrastinate when they hear the call and worship Him beyond their emotions, ensure Jesus Christ has not become an accessory in their life. They know that if they are not careful, He can become a thing to have that makes them look good to the outside world.

Christ bids His disciples to come and follow (Matthew 16:24-26). When I researched the topic of following Jesus Christ, I discovered that there are really three groups of people that follow Him.

First are the crowds. The crowd was fascinated with the new teaching, miracles, feedings and healings. (Matt. 4:25; Mark 1:32-33; John 6:2.) Jesus knew why each person was in His crowd. I often consider the fact that He fed 5,000 (not including the women and children who would have been there), yet about only 120 were in the upper room after his death (Acts 1:15). Where did they all go?

Second, are the curious. The curious come to Him with a statement or question and He provides instructions (Luke 9:57-62; 18:22-23). We don't see where they become converted. In fact, for the most part they depart with no further action.

Third are the disciples. He called them from their preoccupation and said, "Follow me." Without hesitation, each left what he was doing and followed Him. Their actions were immediate and life altering. Simon and Andrew (Matthew 4:18-20); James and John (Mark 1:19-20); Matthew (Matthew 9:9) and Philip (John 1:43). Nathanael was unique because Jesus didn't give him the command to follow Him (John 1:44-49). After a brief encounter, Nathanael recognized Him immediately and, without hesitation, became His disciple.

The cost to follow Jesus was paid immediately by His disciples. They left what they had and joined Him in what He was doing in the earth. Even when they weren't clear about things and were scared, the disciples were still found in the upper room awaiting Pentecost. The half-hearted turned and walked away, never to return to our knowledge. And, the crowds that thronged Him as He ministered were most likely the very same ones who stood before Pilate and shouted, "Let Him be crucified" (Matthew 27:20-22).

Which of the three groups are you in? Have you left your old way of life for a new one found only in Christ? Are you one of the curious without a true conversion? The question for us is, are we willing to pay the cost? Will we follow Jesus because we recognize Him as the Son of God? Is Jesus just that important to you?

Time to Reflect

Scripture: Luke 9:23-26, John 12:26

Observation: What are some of your thoughts about His command, "Follow Me"?

Application: How does this knowledge help you to commit more deeply to following Christ?

Prayer: Pray about any <u>one</u> of the suggested options below. You are not expected to do all three unless the Holy Spirit directs you otherwise.

What can you commit to Jesus?
What do you want Him to do for you?
What do you want Him to help you to do?

Deeper Still: Using a good study Bible with commentary, review these Scriptures: *Matt. 16:24-26; Luke 14:27; John 6:66-68.*

Praise and Worship: What praise or worship song comes to mind as you conclude our devotional for the day? I encourage you to listen to it now. Below is my playlist, which has a variety of artists and genres, so hold on and enjoy it if you care to partake.

"I Have Decided to Follow Jesus" – Lydia Walker – (Lyric Video)[43]
"The True Story Behind The Song–"I Have Decided To Follow Jesus" – SoulJa Of God[44]
"I Believe In A Hill Called Mount Calvary" – Gaither Vocal Band – Live[45]

---

[43] Lydia Walker, "I Have Decided to Follow Jesus (Lyric Video)," uploaded by Lydia Walker, August 11, 2021, YouTube music video, 2:45, https://www.youtube.com/watch?v=L7XHeCZB5KU.

[44] SoulJa Of God, "The True Story Behind The Song "I Have Decided To Follow Jesus," uploaded by SoulJa Of God, April 29, 2017, YouTube music video, 5:23, https://www.youtube.com/watch?v=9mLC2XAXKac.

[45] Gaither Vocal Band, "I Believe In A Hill Called Mount Calvary (Live)," uploaded by Gaither Music TV, November 8, 2012, YouTube music video, 3:45, https://www.youtube.com/watch?v=4NSdy2N7mHA.

WE ARE THE GIFT TO THE SON OF GOD FROM GOD THE FATHER

John 17:24

One year for my birthday, I received a beautiful black box with a red mesh bow. It was elegant and arrived in the mail approximately 10 days prior to my birthday. I placed the beautiful box on an ottoman in my family room and admired it for 10 days. It was a gift, but the box blessed me just as much as the gift inside. As you can see, gifts are exciting for me and I have no problem waiting to open them. I know some of you reading this would have never waited.

One of the most profound theological concepts, which I recently grasped in a deeper, revelatory way, is the relationship and love between God the Father and God the Son. When I first learned that I was a gift to the Son from the Father, I was astonished, humbled and grateful for God's amazing grace. I am that box and the gift inside, given to the Son from the Father. Take a pause break and think about this.

John 17:6 says that we were given to the Son, but before we were given, we belonged to the Father. Salvation is a sovereign act of the Father and not us (Ephesians 2:8-10). In John 6:37, the believer was given to Christ so that we may behold Christ's glory and we were given to the Son before the foundation of the world (Ephesians 1:3-6). We were given – wow, a gift! – it boggles my mind.

Christ's mission was to seek and to save that which was lost (Luke 19:10). He was determined to do the Father's will as it pertained to the lost (John 6:38). What I like about Christ's faithfulness for the gifts the Father has given the Son is that He won't cast us out (John 6:37). He won't lose one of us and He will raise us up on the last day (John 6:39). Jesus keeps us while we are in this world (John 17:12) and He desires that we are with Him (John 17:24).

The passage that knocks me to my knees and brings me great hope and joy is His presentation of me as faultless before the presence of His glory with exceeding joy to the Father (Jude 24). Please stop and think about what this really means! Who wouldn't serve a God like this?

Why is Christ important? He has held my future in ages past! (Ephesians 1:4) Nothing I can do will separate me from the love of God which is in Christ Jesus our Lord (Romans 8:38-39).

Time to Reflect

Scripture: John 17:24

Observation: What are some of your thoughts about being a gift to the Father?

Application: How does this knowledge help you to commit more deeply to the Savior?

Prayer: Pray about any <u>one</u> of the suggested options below. You are not expected to do all three unless the Holy Spirit directs you otherwise.

What can you commit to Jesus?
What do you want Him to do for you?
What do you want Him to help you to do?

Deeper Still: Using a good study Bible with commentary, review these Scriptures: *John 6:44; 6:65; Rom. 8:29-30; Eph. 2:1-10; 1 Pet. 1:2.*

Praise and Worship: What praise or worship song comes to mind as you conclude our devotional for the day? I encourage you to listen to it now. Below is my playlist, which has a variety of artists and genres, so hold on and enjoy it if you care to partake.

"Give Thanks" – Don Moen – Live Worship Sessions[46]
"I Really Want to Worship You My Lord" – Noel Richards[47]
"All I Have Is Christ" – (feat. Paul Baloche) – Official Lyric Video[48]
"Because He Lives" – Guy Penrod[49]

---

[46] Don Moen, "Give Thanks Live Worship Sessions," uploaded by Don Moen TV, July 26, 2017, YouTube music video, 4:23, https://www.youtube.com/watch?v=blbslHDgceY.

[47] Noel Richards, "I Really Want to Worship You My Lord," uploaded by WeAreWorship Lyrics & Chords, March 21, 2017, YouTube music video, 4:38, https://www.youtube.com/watch?v=URIkXQfHUBc.

[48] Sovereign Grace Music, "All I Have Is Christ (feat. Paul Baloche) – Official Lyric Video," uploaded by Sovereign Grace Music, April 21, 2014, YouTube music video, 5:17, https://www.youtube.com/watch?v=ugGucoYMmKg.

[49] Guy Penrod, "Because He Lives," uploaded by Gateway Church TV, November 23, 2017, Youtube music video, 3:37, https://www.youtube.com/watch?v=V2P57HSVzqc.

Week 3: What Makes Christ Special in the Life of A Woman?

"There is nothing in this universe you need more desperately than Christ."
~R.C. Sproul

HE IS WORTHY OF OUR TOTAL DEVOTION

Anna Luke 2:36-38

Anna was totally devoted to God and she is given a voice to proclaim the Christ child to all who would listen. Anna means favor or grace. It almost seems her life doesn't resemble either until you take a closer look. In a two-verse biography, this woman is a powerhouse and an example of the outcome of a heart truly devoted to Christ. Her story begins with loss and devastation. It ends with triumph and satisfaction of a life well spent.

Anna was either 84 or, some believe, as old as 104 when she encounters the Christ child. If she was married at about 14, wedded for seven years, and widowed for 84 years, the age of over a century would be correct. In either case, her age pales in comparison to her actions. What might we learn from this victorious woman?

She serves in her God-given gift. Anna dared to be different. The Scriptures tell us that one of her roles was as a prophetess, a woman who proclaimed the Scriptures from the Old Testament. This was quite unusual for a woman of her day, yet the Lord put this gift in her heart. And she proclaimed the Word of the Lord to all who would listen.

She displays a grateful character. Anna's character exuded a devotion to God which proceeded a heart filled with gratitude. The Scripture says she came in that instant and gave thanks to the Lord. Thankfulness is an expression of the overflow of one's heart. Who we spend time with and how we spend our time has a direct relationship to the wellspring of our heart in every situation.

She has a God-controlled nature. We see that Anna was a woman that was God-controlled and not self-controlled. She served God night and day, fasting and praying with an expectation that God would fulfill His promise for the redemption of Jerusalem (Luke 2:38).

Her early loss did not derail her. Years of devotion were spent learning, teaching, hoping, proclaiming and waiting. This time of obscurity allowed her to develop into a mature image bearer of God Himself. By the grace and favor on her life, Anna would become the first woman to herald the good news that the Savior, the Christ child, had come. In the wait, Christ had shaped and molded her into a bold vessel that was prepared to witness from the wellspring of her heart about the special gift we have in Christ. She was not scared to openly proclaim to all, yes all, who looked for redemption in Israel.

You, like Anna, may have a derailment or two in your life. Are you prepared to follow in the footsteps of Anna and devote your life fully to Christ? Will you let Him shape you into His image?

Time to Reflect

Scripture: Luke 2:36-38

Observation: What are some of your thoughts about what made Christ special to Anna?

Application: How does this knowledge help you to commit more deeply to Christ knowing that He could return any day?

Prayer: Pray about any <u>one</u> of the suggested options below. You are not expected to do all three unless the Holy Spirit directs you otherwise.

What can you commit to Jesus?
What do you want Him to do for you?
What do you want Him to help you to do?

Deeper Still: Using a good study Bible with commentary, review these Scriptures of other women in scripture that proclaimed God's Word to His people: Miriam *(Exodus 15:20)*; Deborah *(Judges 4:4)*; Huldah *(2 Kings. 22:14; 2 Chron. 34:22)*; and Philip's daughters *(Acts 21:9)*.

Praise and Worship: What praise or worship song comes to mind as you conclude our devotional for the day? I encourage you to listen to it now. Below is my playlist, which has a variety of artists and genres, so hold on and enjoy it if you care to partake.

"Have Thine Own Way" – Lynda Randle[50]
"Take My Hand, Precious Lord" – Marshall Hall, Angela Primm, Jason Crabb[51]
"My Soul Says Yes" – Sonnie Badu – (Official Live Recording)[52]
"Is He Worthy?" – Chris Tomlin – (Live)[53]

---

[50] Lynda Randle, "Have Thine Own Way," provided by Universal Music Group, July 29, 2018, YouTube music video, 3:12, https://www.youtube.com/watch?v=FKIdMtr08FE.

[51] Marshall Hall, Angela Primm, Jason Crabb, "Take My Hand, Precious Lord (Live)," uploaded by Gaither Music TV, July 11, 2012, YouTube music video, 6:37, https://www.youtube.com/watch?v=RaF16IlysQc.

[52] Sonnie Badu, "My Soul Says Yes (Official Live Recording)," uploaded by Official Sonnie Badu TV, October 9, 2016, YouTube music video, 9:09, https://www.youtube.com/watch?v=_Vuw0o0CXLI.

[53] Chris Tomlin, "Is He Worthy? (Live)," uploaded by Chris Tomlin Music, Official Live Video, February 1, 2019, YouTube music video, 6:56, https://www.youtube.com/watch?v=FkRiYsTN7KY

HE EXPOSES OUR FAITH TO A DYING WORLD AND WILL PUT OUR FAITH ON BLAST

The Woman of Canaan Matthew 15:21-28; Mark 7:24-30

The woman of Canaan was faithful and focused. She knew what she wanted from the Master and she was persistent. Here she was, a Greek in both her language and religion, a Syro-Phoenician by birth (Mark 7:26), a descendant of the Canaanites (Matthew 15:22) and a complete outsider before the Jewish Savior. She didn't let her history, ethnicity or religion get in her way. She was not a victim, she was a woman on a mission. She took two actions. First, she heard about this new teacher. Next, she came to the Christ, this Jesus of Galilee, who was the only one who could address her problem. She humbled herself at this foreigner's feet (Mark 7:25).

In Matthew 15:22, she cried out with a command and a characterization. Even though she was interceding on behalf of her daughter, her command was, "Have mercy on me." Her characterization was the use of His royal title, "O Lord, Son of David!" Besides hearing and coming to Christ, she humbled herself and asked. Mark 7:26 says she kept asking Him to cast the demon out of her daughter. This woman was suffering because of the plight of her child. She was relentless and focused, interceding on her daughter's behalf.

According to Lockyer, "Her conquering faith exhibited the three ascending degrees of all true faith. The trial of her faith consisted of silence (Matthew 15:23), refusal (Matthew 15:24) and reproach (Matthew 15: 26), all of which were intended by Christ for a beneficent, loving purpose." (Lockyer) In the face of seeming opposition from the Savior Himself, she was not deterred.

Did you notice? What I love most about this role model for my walk in Christ is her maturity. She was not easily offended (Psalm 119:165). She didn't walk away offended, hurt, bruised and vowing never to return when Christ told her that it is not good to take the children's bread and throw it to the little dogs (Matthew 15:26). This heroine of the faith remained steadfast as she agreed with Him. Here comes her demonstration of faith, which will ring through the portals of the ages. It will be put on blast by Jesus Himself for all to see. She said, "Yes Lord, yet even the little dogs eat the crumbs which fall from their masters' table" (Matthew 15:27). With this statement Jesus says to her, "... O woman, great is your faith! Let it be to you as you desire" (Matthew 15:28). When she arrived home, her daughter was free of her demon possession (Mark 7:30).

Think about what you may be facing. Can Jesus demonstrate why He is special, by exposing your faith in Him, through your trial or life situation? In other words, can He put your faith and focus on blast as He did for this woman? How mature are you? Are you overly sensitive and easily offended?

Time to Reflect

Scripture: Matt. 15:21-28; Mark 7:24-30

Observation: What are some of your thoughts about this focused and faithful woman?

Application: How does this knowledge help you to commit more deeply to Christ?

Prayer: Pray about any <u>one</u> of the suggested options below. You are not expected to do all three unless the Holy Spirit directs you otherwise.

What can you commit to Jesus?
What do you want Him to do for you?
What do you want Him to help you to do?

Deeper Still: Using a good study Bible with commentary, review these Scriptures of others who went to the Master with differing results: *Luke 9:57-60; Luke 18:23; Mark 10:17- 22; John 6:60-67; Mark 9:23-24; John 6:36; John 13:11.* From your point of view, what makes this woman of Canaan stand out?

Praise and Worship: What praise or worship song comes to mind as you conclude our devotional for the day? I encourage you to listen to it now. Below is my playlist, which has a variety of artists and genres, so hold on and enjoy it if you care to partake.

"Almighty, I Surrender" – Damaris Carbaugh[54]
"O Lord My Rock and My Redeemer" –– T4G Live IV [Official Lyric Video] – Sovereign Grace Music[55]
"Wonderful, Merciful Savior" – Grace Larson[56]
"There Is Something About That Name [Live]" – Gaither Vocal Band[57]

---

54 Damaris Carbaugh, "Almighty, I Surrender," provided by CDBaby, July 8, 2015, YouTube music video, 4:39, https://www.youtube.com/watch?v=wiQUmwOAI64.

55 Sovereign Grace Music, "O Lord My Rock and My Redeemer – T4G Live IV [Official Lyric Video]," uploaded by Sovereign Grace Music, March 31, 2020, YouTube music video, 5:18, https://www.youtube.com/watch?v=TxC16duiHvQ.

56 Grace Larson, "Wonderful, Merciful Savior," uploaded by Bryan Bryan T, Family Worship Center in Baton Rouge, LA, April 30, 2017, YouTube music video, 7:48, https://www.youtube.com/watch?v=AFIAeNKyBoo.

57 Gaither Vocal Band, "There Is Something About That Name [Live]," uploaded by Gaither Music TV, August 23, 2012, YouTube music video, 4:58, https://www.youtube.com/watch?v=SdSl9ynS3G4.

HE CALLS HIS DAUGHTERS BY HIS MATCHLESS GRACE

True Grace Girls – Elizabeth and Mary Luke 1:23-25, 26-45, 46-55

Elizabeth means 'God is my oath.' Oath means promise, pledge, vow or assurance. Mary means obstinacy. Obstinacy means stubbornness, determination, wrongheadedness, pigheadedness, inflexibility, unreasonableness or persistence. This cursory examination of the synonyms of the two primary meanings of their names in my word processor, led me to surmise that these girls were set up from birth to be the original "Grace Girls." The meaning of their names, oath and obstinacy, reflect how graciously Elizabeth and Mary handled the circumstances in their lives.

Grace is God's unmerited favor and kindness toward humanity. A Grace Girl walks in the favor of God no matter what may come. In Luke 1:6, Elizabeth is described as righteous, walking in all the commandments and ordinances of the Lord and simply blameless. Like most Grace Girls, Elizabeth has a problem. She has the humiliating social stigma of barrenness. While she is blameless before God, she is experiencing man's judgment for her barrenness, which is culturally presumed to be the disfavor of God. To add insult to injury, she is well advanced in age and most likely well past the normal childbearing years. Of course, this is where grace does its best work. Where is that, you ask? In the center of our need.

Her husband's prayers are answered (Luke 1:13). Elizabeth is to have a son and by divine decree his name is to be John. Now, John means, 'Jehovah has shown grace!' When Zacharias is finished ministering in the temple, he goes home and this Grace Girl conceives. What joy must have filled their home in anticipation of God's gracious oath, promise and vow.

Meanwhile, the teenager Mary receives a visit from God's angel Gabriel. In Luke 1:26, Gabriel tells her to rejoice, highly favored one (a.k.a. Grace Girl) the Lord is with you. He tells her she will conceive, have a son and his name is to be Jesus, which means God is salvation. Mary asks how this can be since she hasn't known a man (Luke 1:34). Gabriel explains what will happen and he concludes by telling her, 'with God nothing will be impossible.' In Luke 1:38, Mary says (obstinately, I might add), *"Let it be to me according to your word."*

What we see about these original Grace Girls is that in the face of unusual circumstances, they trusted God. They both stood on the word they were given. They both were blessed and favored. In Elizabeth's case, a delay for most of her life did not mean a denial. For Mary, a visitation from an angel, coupled with her unyielding and inflexible faith would catapult her into the annals of time. Oh, one final thing about these Grace Girls. The grace of God caused them to worship. When they came together, they put a praise on it (Luke 1:41-55)! Christ was special to these two Grace Girls.

Time to Reflect

Scripture: Luke 1:23-25; 26-45; 46-55

Observation: What are some of your thoughts about the amazing grace God showed Elizabeth and Mary?

Application: How does this knowledge help you to commit more deeply to Jesus our Savior?

Prayer: Pray about any <u>one</u> of the suggested options below. You are not expected to do all three unless the Holy Spirit directs you otherwise.

What can you commit to Jesus?
What do you want Him to do for you?
What do you want Him to help you to do?

Deeper Still: Using a good study Bible with commentary, review these Scriptures about God's saving grace: *Rom. 3:24; 11:6; Eph. 2:5; Titus 2:11; 3:7; 1 Peter 2:1-3.*

Praise and Worship: What praise or worship song comes to mind as you conclude - our devotional for the day? I encourage you to listen to it now. Below is my playlist, which has a variety of artists and genres, so hold on and enjoy it if you care to partake.

"I'm Gonna Put A Praise On It" – Tasha Cobbs (Audio/W Lyrics) – One Place Live[58]
"Grace Greater Than Our Sin" – Don Moen[59]
"Were It Not For Grace" – Chuck Arrington[60]
"Marvelous" – Walter Hawkins 25th Anniversary Reunion[61]

---

[58] Tasha Cobbs, "I'm Gonna Put A Praise On It (Audio/W Lyrics) – One Place Live," Uploaded by Soulful Gospel Music TV, March 30, 2016, YouTube music video, 6:16, https://www.youtube.com/watch?v=4cSgovCdUcE.

[59] Don Moen, "Grace Greater Than Our Sin," uploaded by DonMoen TV, June 2, 2017, YouTube music video, 3:19, https://www.youtube.com/watch?v=xdUDqKIIQxM.

[60] Chuck Arrington, "Were It Not For Grace," uploaded by Josiah Birai, May 24, 2021, YouTube music video, 4:38, https://www.youtube.com/watch?v=6qoAf72zVDs.

[61] Walter Hawkins, "Marvelous," provided by Tune Core, June 19, 2014, Walter Hawkins and the Love Center Choir Love Alive V 25th Anniversary Reunion CD, YouTube music video, 7:36, https://www.youtube.com/watch?v=t4aIFXpgTyE.

WHEN WE ARE DEAD WRONG, HE CAN MAKE US DEAD RIGHT

The Woman Caught In Adultery John 8:1-11

This woman is not known by her religion, geography or faithfulness. She is brought to the Master because she has been "caught" in the very act of her sin. She has no name, just a sin-stained present that demands the verdict of death.

Can you see her standing before truth (John 14:6), the Holy One of Israel, with her head hung low? Caught and fully exposed to pure holiness (Mark 1:24). Her adversaries are accusing, condemning and demanding justice for this evil, nasty and illicit woman. They have the Law of Moses on their side. They are right! She is, as my mother used to say, "as wrong as two left shoes." She is standing there in the balance of life and death. Her self-condemnation is most likely screaming just as strongly as the voices of her accusers, "You deserve this. You ought to be ashamed of yourself. You knew better. This is what you deserve." On top of them and her own self-condemnation there is the law and there is no forgiveness for what she has done. The penalty for her crime is most certainly stoning.

Ashamed, embarrassed and guilty, perhaps even longing for death at this very moment, she has no human way of escape. Here she is, set before the presence of the most righteous judge (John 5:22). While she is wrong, she is swept up into a Pharisaical test which has more to do with them trying to entrap Jesus and less to do with her. Jesus, the Son of the living God, just ignores her accusers and writes on the ground.

Then He speaks, and she hears a proverbial link in the chain of her sinful life fall to the ground. Can you hear it go clink? In John 8:7 Jesus says,"*He who is without sin among you, let him throw a stone at her first.*" Their self-righteousness begins to melt, from the oldest even to the last, the Scripture says. While the Bible doesn't explicitly say this, presumably, stones begin to drop one by one as their consciences begin to convict them (John 8:9). She is left alone with Jesus – clank, her proverbial chain is totally loose now–and He inquires about her accusers.

You may be just like this woman, dead wrong. No matter what your past; drugs, prostitution, abortion, murder, child abuse, child molestation, lesbianism, self-righteousness, nasty attitude, religious condemning spirit, condescending, Miss Perfect and the list goes on... No matter what! Jesus asks you the same question He asked this woman. "Has no one condemned you ... Neither do I condemn you; go and sin no more." Her sinful past and our sinful pasts are not beyond his salvation power. If we go to Jesus and confess our sins, He will cleanse and forgive us (1 John 1:9; Ephesians 4:32; Colossians 2:13; Romans 10:9-11).

This is what makes Jesus Christ special. He can take our dead wrong situations and cleanse us from all unrighteousness. Don't make your accusers bigger than

Christ. Don't let Satan, your accuser, stand in the way of you receiving healing and forgiveness from the true judge (John 1:12).

So let's review. This woman is wrong. The Pharisees are trying to really catch Jesus in the wrong. Jesus, who is always right, rights her wrong. We serve a God that makes our wrongs right if we let Him. Will you take a posture of bringing the wrong in your life to Him?

Time to Reflect

Scripture: John 8:1-11

Observation: What are some of your thoughts about how God rights our wrongs?

Application: How does this knowledge help you to understand the necessity of Jesus in your life today?

Prayer: Pray about any <u>one</u> of the suggested options below. You are not expected to do all three unless the Holy Spirit directs you otherwise.

What can you commit to Jesus?
What do you want Him to do for you?
What do you want Him to help you to do?

Deeper Still: Using a good study Bible with commentary, review Peter's forgiveness experience and restoration in *Mark 14:66-72* and *John 21:15-19*. Next, review Saul's experience in *Acts 9:1-19*.

Praise and Worship: What praise or worship song comes to mind as you conclude our devotional for the day? I encourage you to listen to it now. Below is my playlist, which has a variety of artists and genres, so hold on and enjoy it if you care to partake.

"I Believe In A Hill Called Mount Calvary" – Gaither Vocal Band – (Live/Lyric Video)[62]
"He Has Forgiven Me" – Damaris Carbaugh[63]
"He's Been Faithful" –The Brooklyn Tabernacle Choir[64]

---

62 Gaither Vocal Band, "I Believe In A Hill Called Mount Calvary (Live/Lyric Video)," uploaded by Gaither Music TV, May 26, 2017, YouTube music video, 3:45, https://www.youtube.com/watch?v=66Qq6yjFEBA.

63 Damaris Carbaugh, "He Has Forgiven Me," provided by CDBaby, July 13, 2015, YouTube music video, 4:56, https://www.youtube.com/watch?v=i6L0N4i2W4Y.

64 The Brooklyn Tabernacle Choir, "He's Been Faithful," uploaded by Marcelo Barrera, January 29, 2017, YouTube music video, 5:26, https://www.youtube.com/watch?v=ymiZ2xB-AfU.

HE USES US AS AN OBJECT LESSON OF HIS AMAZING GRACE

Used by the Master – A Sinful Woman Luke 7:36-50

Let's set the record straight before we begin this devotional. This is not the same woman who is recorded in Matthew, Mark and John as anointing Jesus' feet. There are two incidents in the Gospels that are quite similar, yet strikingly different. Review our passages in the Deeper Still Section for greater understanding. For now, trust me; this story is a unique one of an entirely different event from that of Mary anointing Christ for His burial, found in Matthew, Mark and John.

The woman in our story today is only known by her human sin-stained inheritance and behavior (Luke 7:37). We don't know her name or what she has done. This woman's sin is left unknown by our writer Luke. Simon the Pharisee (Luke 7:40), whose house she visits, characterizes her as a "manner of woman." The meaning of "manner" in Greek is that she was a "sought of woman," or "a kind of woman." This has led some scholars to believe she was a prostitute and further surmise that she is Mary Magdalene. However, other scholars don't believe this is Mary Magdalene, since she is not mentioned in Scripture until Luke 8:2, after this story. In any case, believe it or not, she is not the point of the story. She is only the object of the lesson. The Pharisee is the main character and the point of Jesus' ministry outreach. The woman was already forgiven, as we will see.

My first question is this: "Can God use your past as an object lesson for others? Do you love Him enough to humble yourself and put your love for Him on display to a dying world?" Let me provide more context. In Luke 6:7, the Pharisees are looking for a way to accuse Jesus. It seems that Simon invites Him to his house to figure out, who he really is. Note his conclusion of the matter, "This man if He were a prophet, would know ..." Simon believes Jesus is not a prophet at all. This Simon, a religious leader and Pharisee who thinks he has it all together, doesn't realize who is in his house. Ah, but the woman who is willing to expose her past for the Master's use knows full well who is in the host's house, even when he does not.

Christ's gracious object lesson, this sinful woman, knows exactly who He is. She has been forgiven for her many sins and she loves much (Luke 7:47). So, let's look at five principles we can learn from her:

Principle 1. Her shameful past doesn't stop her future.

This woman first learns that Jesus is at Simon's house. She goes to where He is, not allowing what others know about her to hinder her purpose. At this point, she is not holding on to the shame of her past (v.36). Are you willing to show up and allow Jesus to use your sinful past? Or are you like Simon, evaluating people on who they used to be and withholding grace from them? Are there some people you wouldn't be caught touching and you wouldn't dare let touch you?

Principle 2. She brings something to the Master.

Look at her. She doesn't come to Him empty handed (v.36). She brings oil from her God-given resources to anoint Him. What God-given resources are you using to anoint those within your circle for Jesus?

Principle 3. She is broken at His feet.

She does what religious Simon neglected to do; she washes, wipes, kisses and anoints His feet, all the while with a deep emotional tearful display (v. 38). The word "weep" in the Greek has the sense of bawling. She doesn't care what others think or say. She just desires to be at His feet! Do you really love the Savior and are you keenly aware that your sins are many, but you have been forgiven much (v.47)? Will you allow God to use you as an object lesson?

Principle 4. She understands His amazing redemptive power–grace.

Her brokenness before the Master is born out of the knowledge of God's raw amazing grace, which she could never earn (Ephesians 2:8-10). Do you understand God's amazing grace and redemptive power (Galatians 3:13) of salvation in your life today?

Principle 5. Our work for God is not so we can be forgiven. What pours out of us is because we are already forgiven.

Her display of brokenness and gratitude were not so she could be forgiven, but because she had already been forgiven (v. 47). Remember, she is an object lesson for Simon. Christ's declaration that her sins are forgiven, her faith had saved her and that she was to go in peace (vv. 48, 50) was for the benefit of this unconverted religious Pharisee who likely invited Him to dinner to trap Him. This woman is an easy object lesson for the Lord because she whole heartedly loves Him and is not ashamed or caring about what others think. What about you?

Are you a sinful woman, saved by grace? Are you in the right place at the right time to be used as His object lesson for what true grace and redemption looks like? Are you willing to look for opportunities where God can use your past to expose another person's sinful condition?

Scripture: Luke 7:36-50

Observation: What are some of your thoughts about the how God used this "sinful" woman?

Application: How does this knowledge help you to understand how Christ may use you today?

Prayer: Pray about any <u>one</u> of the suggested options below. You are not expected to do all three unless the Holy Spirit directs you otherwise.

What can you commit to Jesus?
What do you want Him to do for you?
What do you want Him to help you to do?

Deeper Still: Using a good study Bible with commentary, review the other story of Mary who anoints His feet for burial, noting the similarities and differences in both stories. That story is found in: *Matthew 26:6-12; Mark 14: 3-9; John 12:1-8.* The Simon in the story not featured in today's devotional is a leper *(Matthew 26:6).* History tells us that no self- righteous Pharisee would ever be caught in the house of a leper. This is one key reason why scholars conclude these are different incidents.

Praise and Worship: What praise or worship song comes to mind as you conclude our devotional for the day? I encourage you to listen to it now. Below is my playlist, which has a variety of artists and genres, so hold on and enjoy it if you care to partake.

"Friend of A Wounded Heart" – Damaris Carbaugh[65]
"Jesus I Love You" – The Brooklyn Tabernacle Choir – Live[66]
"Jesus, There's No One Like You" – Prayers of the Saints Live – Sovereign Grace Music[67]
"Gratitude"–Vanessa Burge Garner[68]

---

65 Damaris Carbaugh, "Friend of A Wounded Heart," provided by CDBaby, July 24, 2015, YouTube music video, 4:46, https://www.youtube.com/watch?v=KvT6X8fpSGQ.

66 The Brooklyn Tabernacle Choir, "Jesus I Love You (Live)," provided by TuneCore, October 10, 2019, YouTube music video, 6:20, https://www.youtube.com/watch?v=QdEOUWoELhs.

67 Sovereign Grace Music, "Jesus, There's No One Like You – Prayers of the Saints Live," uploaded by ChaNel Lyric Videos, April 14, 2021, YouTube music video, 4:26, https://www.youtube.com/watch?v=9kjqMKFgfo0.

68 Vanessa Burge Garner, "Gratitude," provided by CDBaby, June 22, 2017, YouTube music video, 4:30, https://www.youtube.com/watch?v=QvJ4i-Vlx1k.

HIS ATTRIBUTES ARE ALWAYS ON DISPLAY IN OUR LIFE

A Woman with the Issue of Blood Mark 5:25-34

Even if you have been in church for just a short period of time, you have most likely heard about this woman. Her story is found in the Synoptic Gospels[69]. She is known only by her physical ailment. She has a flow of blood that can't be stopped. This issue renders her ceremonially unclean (Leviticus 15:25-27; 31-33) and socially isolated. She can't go to the synagogue or the temple. She is excluded from the daily life of her community. She is thrust into a place of seclusion and despair.

She has done all she can to seek healing from her problem. She has spent all her money, over a 12-year period, to no avail. This woman doesn't get any better, in fact, Mark 5:26 tells us she gets worse. Anyone coming in contact with her would be considered unclean. What a miserable existence. Can you imagine how she must have felt? Frustrated, depressed, lonely, aggravated and isolated from her family and friends. She is cast out, but not down for the count. Let's examine her actions.

Luke 8:44 tells us that she hears about Jesus and comes from behind in the crowd and touches the hem of His garment. MacArthur indicates that when she touched Him, what would have normally rendered anyone else unclean produced precisely the opposite effect. She becomes clean (MacArthur, 1997)! This is what Christ does for all His daughters. He is able and wants to make us clean. There are three attributes of Jesus the Christ in her life and ours:

First, He demonstrates His omniscient and sovereign will
There is a moment in the exchange between her touch of the cloth and her healing where His healing virtue leaves Him by His sovereign will (Mark 5:30). In other words, He allowed her healing to be so. Make no mistake, Jesus was not confused by what happened. His question as to who touched His clothes was for the benefit of the woman and the crowd. Her public confession of the inward healing (Mark 5:29) was to be used to express and praise Him outwardly. Do you think she gave Him the glory and told her testimony everywhere she went? What about you? Where has Jesus been omniscient and sovereign in your life? Are you telling others?

Second, He is her Prince of Peace
He commands her to go in peace (Mark 5:34). We have seen this week that the Prince of Peace (Isaiah 9:6) has given two of His daughters this sweet kiss of peace. He commands her and the sinful woman from yesterday (Luke 7:50) to go in peace. Jesus can heal us, too, and we can walk in His peace.

---

[69] The Synoptic Gospels are the three gospels- Matthew, Mark and Luke – which through each has distinctive emphasis; they approach the life of Christ from basically similar positions. (Erickson, 2001)

Third, He is her savior

Jesus is the only bridge between us and God the Father. No one else can make us well physically and spiritually. The Greek word for "well" in Matthew 9:22; Mark 5:34 and Luke 8:48 literally means to deliver, save, keep from harm, preserve or rescue. The sense in the Greek is that this woman's healing was not only physical, but spiritual. The physical healing authenticates Him as the Son of God (Mark 6:2; John 3:2; John 5:36; John 7:31). Reaching for the hem of His garment, while believing Him to be the Son of God, spiritually healed her for eternity (John 5:24, 21). In His outflow, He becomes her savior.

Time to Reflect
_____

Scripture: Mark 5:25-34

Observation: What are some of your thoughts about who Christ is in this woman's difficult situation?

Application: How does this knowledge draw you closer to Jesus?

Prayer: Pray about any <u>one</u> of the suggested options below. You are not expected to do all three unless the Holy Spirit directs you otherwise.

What can you commit to Jesus?
What do you want Him to do for you?
What do you want Him to help you to do?

Deeper Still: Using a good study Bible with commentary, review the other passages that cover this story: *Matt. 9:20-22; Luke 8:43-48.* Also, review the Omniscience of Christ in *John 16:30; John 21:17;* Christ's Peace in *Isa. 53:5; Rom. 5:1; Eph. 2:14;* and Christ as Savior in *Acts 4:12; Luke 2:30; 19:10; Acts 5:31.*

Praise and Worship: What praise or worship song comes to mind as you conclude our devotional for the day? I encourage you to listen to it now. Below is my playlist, which has a variety of artists and genres, so hold on and enjoy it if you care to partake.

"Touch the Hem of His Garment" – Sam Cooke with the Soul Stirrers[70]
"Faith"- Vanessa Burge Garner[71]
"Oh It Is Jesus" – Tata Vega[72]

---

[70] Sam Cooke with the Soul Stirrers, "Touch The Hem Of His Garment," provided by Universal Music Group, December 2, 2018, YouTube music video, 2:02, https://www.youtube.com/watch?v=NfhEE7NPVjY.

[71] Vanessa Burge Garner, "Faith," provided by CDBaby, June 22, 2017, YouTube music video, 5:10, https://www.youtube.com/watch?v=TyLQ5fQ_LK8.

[72] Tata Vega, "Oh It Is Jesus," provided by Rhino/Warner Records, January 23, 2017, YouTube music video, 5:04, https://www.youtube.com/watch?v=lBHTd5XtNIM.

HE DESERVES OUR WORSHIP – HE IS THE MESSIAH

The Woman at the Well John 4:25-26

A shunned woman. She was isolated from the other women who went to the well. This woman had a history with men. Were they all husbands who died? Were they husbands who had divorced her? Were they husbands who had abandoned or separated from her? The Bible doesn't tell us. All we know is that she had five of them and the one she was currently with was not her own (John 4:17-18).

History tells us this woman would have been considered by the Jews as unclean. Samaritans were despised by both Jews and Gentiles, yet Jesus, out of obligation and necessity, went through the territory of the Samaritans to meet this woman. He crossed ethnic and religious boundaries to meet her. As we listen to the conversation we learn that this woman was smart. She revealed that she knew her history (vv.12,22) and the place where her people were to worship (v. 20). Furthermore, she was theologically astute and had knowledge of the Messiah who would come and tell them all things (v. 25). Unfortunately, her knowledge and theology would not bring her eternal life. And sadly, many of our own thoughts and understanding of who Christ is could have us miss the hope of glory as Paul describes in Colossians 1:27. Think about what you know and understand about Jesus. Will it save you and give you eternal life? Do you believe what the Bible says about Him? How do you know you are saved?

As you meditate on our devotion for today, question what you think and believe. Ask yourself, do I understand what Jesus meant when He said clearly that He was the Messiah in v. 26? There are three things Jesus declares about Himself and the Father that are worth examining:

First, He will give you living water (John 4: 10, 13). The result of the living water that Christ gives is characteristic of a resurrected life in Him. When we experience the Savior's water, which John later describes as the Holy Spirit, we will never thirst again (John 7:37-39).

Second, God is Spirit (John 4:24). God is Spirit. He has no physical image, yet he shares with His creation His moral attributes (Genesis 1:27-27). We are made in the very likeness of Him. The worship of God is not to be confined to location such as in Jerusalem or on a mountain as she thought (v.20). True worship will come from within based on the truth of who Christ is in your life.

Third, worship is to be in spirit and in truth. John 4:23 says, "... true worshippers will worship the Father in spirit and truth; for the Father is seeking such to worship Him." When we are in Christ, our worship becomes an inward expression and manifestation of our encounter with His Word and who He is. When a person has only a little Word in them, their worship will lack authenticity because the person really doesn't know Him. Worship for this person is difficult because of a lack of the Word. Genuine worship flows from our heart and soul to the throne room of God (Ps. 119:34; Jer. 29:13; Matt. 22:37). It is God-centered and not man-centered. Worship from the heart and a renewed mind will reflect our redemptive encounter with the Messiah and the new nature He has given us (Gal. 2:20, 2 Cor. 5:17). The outpouring of this woman's heart includes her leaving her water pot, going to the men of the city and witnessing to them, "Come see a man." True worship did not have her in a specific place. True worship had her spirit in action, proclaiming and asking, "Could this be the Christ?" (vv. 28-29)

What about you? Is your spirit actively worshiping God with the truth from His Word? Are you excited about telling others what you know about the Messiah?

Time to Reflect
_____

Scripture: John 4:25-26

Observation: What are some of your thoughts about the fact that Jesus is the Messiah?

Application: What does Jesus' Messiahship mean to you and how do you know you worship Him in spirit and truth?

Prayer: Pray about any <u>one</u> of the suggested options below. You are not expected to do all three unless the Holy Spirit directs you otherwise.

What can you commit to Jesus?
What do you want Him to do for you?
What do you want Him to help you to do?

Deeper Still: Using a good study Bible with commentary, review these passages, which tie in to today's devotional: *Isa. 12:3; 44:3; Joel 2:12; Matt. 2:2, 11; 14:33; 28:9; 28:17; Luke 24:52; John 9:31; Phil. 3:3; 2:10-11; Heb. 1:6; Rev. 5:8.*

Praise and Worship: What praise or worship song comes to mind as you conclude our devotional for the day? I encourage you to listen to it now. Below is my playlist, which has a variety of artists and genres, so hold on and enjoy it if you care to partake.

"Fill My Cup Lord" – Angie Primm – Live[73]
"The Well" – Casting Crowns – w/Lyrics[74]

_____

[73] Angie Primm, "Fill My Cup, Lord (Live)," provided by Gaither Music TV, February 7, 2013, YouTube music video, 3:46, https://www.youtube.com/watch?v=_8ykaEdfiZ4.

[74] Casting Crowns, "The Well," uploaded by FollowingHimToday, October 18, 2011, YouTube music video, 5:04, https://www.youtube.com/watch?v=bW5unzXXC0k.

Week 4: Compelled to Tell About My Jesus!

"And He has on His robe
and on His thigh a name written:
Jesus Christ, KING OF KINGS AND LORD
OF LORDS."
Revelation 19:16

IT IS SETTLED – HE IS LORD!

Philippians 2:10–11

Good news, good news! Consider the last time you received good news. How exciting to learn that something you longed for and hoped for has come to fruition. Take a moment to consider some of the good news you like to receive. Is it an unexpected check in the mail? Perhaps, it's a promotion. What about the news that a baby is on the way? He proposed. Your loved one you have been praying with and for is healed. You go back to the doctor and they can't find what was once on the x-ray. You might be smiling right now and mentally basking in that last bit of good news you received. The point is–we all love good news.

Our Scripture today has the best news ever given to mankind – "...Jesus Christ is Lord, to the glory of God the Father" (Phil. 2:11). Men and women, no matter where they are in the heavens, in the earth or under the earth, will confess (acknowledge, affirm or agree), in praise or duress, that Jesus is Lord. The word Lord in this passage means ruler or one who commands. As Christ's title, it also means, "One who exercises supernatural authority over mankind." (Louw)

This is the logical conclusion Paul comes to because of Christ's actions in Philippians 2:6-8. Jesus took two significant actions which resulted in humanity's confession of Him as Lord. First, He made Himself of no reputation (Philippians 2:7) and second, He humbled Himself (Philippians 2:8).

His actions are momentous because being in the form of God (meaning He was God), He took the form of a bondservant (slave) and He, the very God of the universe, came in the likeness of men (Philippians 2:7). Wait, He didn't stop there. In the same verse, it says He became obedient to the point of death on the cross.

Now stop for a moment and meditate on these passages. Really think about what this is saying. God Himself, did all this for you and me, "...while we are still sinners ...(Rom. 5:8). In the words of Pastor John K. Jenkins Sr., "Ushers, guard the doors, because someone is going to jump up and run out of here!" At this point, we should be shouting, crying and overflowing with genuine gratitude for Jesus Christ. We should be excited to go and tell someone today about what He has done in our lives. Who in your life needs to hear today why Jesus Christ is your Lord?

Time to Reflect

Scripture: Philippians 2:10-11

Observation: What are some of your thoughts about Christ's title–Lord?

Application: What does Christ's Lordship mean to you?

Prayer: Pray about any <u>one</u> of the suggested options below. You are not expected to do all three unless the Holy Spirit directs you otherwise.

What can you commit to the Lord Jesus?
What do you want Him to do for you?
What do you want Him to help you to do?

Deeper Still: Using a good study Bible with commentary, review these other passages that cover Jesus Christ our Lord: *Mark 2:28; Luke 1:32; 2:11; 24:34; John 13:13; Acts 10:36; Rom. 10:9; 14:9; 1 Cor. 12:3; Eph. 1:21; Heb. 2:8; Rev. 19:6.*

Praise and Worship: What praise or worship song comes to mind as you conclude our devotional for the day? I encourage you to listen to it now. Below is my playlist, which has a variety of artists and genres, so hold on and enjoy it if you care to partake.

"He is Lord" – Alvin Slaughter – Overcomer DVD[75]
"Victory Belongs to Jesus"–Todd Dulaney–(Lyrics)[76]
"How Excellent" – Mississippi Choir[77]
"Knowing You Worship Song"–Kendrick Graham[78]

---

[75] Alvin Slaughter, "He Is Lord," provided by Absolute Marketing International Ltd., September 21, 2015, Youtube music video, 3:07, https://www.youtube.com/watch?v=25KQeFYqhJU.

[76] Todd Dulaney, "Victory Belongs to Jesus (Lyrics)," uploaded by Song of Solomon Ministries, November 20, 2016, YouTube music video, 5:58, https://www.youtube.com/watch?v=IkASX8Fd1tE.

[77] Mississippi Mass Choir, "How Excellent," uploaded by Kleavell20, June 4, 2012, YouTube music video, 5:28, https://www.youtube.com/watch?v=W17-4LDYH74.

[78] Graham Kendrick, "Knowing You - Worship Song by Graham Kendrick from Philippians 3," uploaded by Graham Kendrick Music, March 21, 2019, YouTube Music Video, 4:43, https://www.youtube.com/watch?v=4r8XfE_VNb0.

HE IS EITHER ... LIAR, LUNATIC OR LORD

Matthew 26:57-68

Born in 1898, Clive Staples Lewis, better known as C.S. Lewis to most of us, was a professor and prolific writer in 20th century England. He is known for his conversion from atheism to Christianity. A master at allegorical writing, he is considered by many to be a literary intellectual genius and is widely quoted. One of his more popular quotes in Apologetic circles is the one below. Please allow me to quote him in context:

"I am trying here to prevent anyone saying that really foolish thing that people often say about Him: I'm ready to accept Jesus as a great moral teacher, but I don't accept his claim to be God. That is the one thing we must not say. A man who was merely a man and said the sort of things Jesus said would not be a great moral teacher. He would either be a lunatic – on the level with the man who says he is a poached egg – or else he would be the Devil of hell. You must make your choice. Either this man was, and is the Son of God, or else a madman or something worse. You can shut him up for a fool, you can spit at him and kill him as a demon or you can fall at his feet and call him Lord and God, but let us not come with any patronizing nonsense about his being a great human teacher. He has not left that open to us. He did not intend to." (Lewis)

C.S. Lewis, Mere Christianity

Now, let's examine Christ before the Sanhedrin in our text for today. Keeping with Lewis' quote, Jesus confirmed for the High-Priest that He was the Christ (Anointed One), the Son of God (Matthew 26:63-64). Was He telling the truth or was He fibbing, telling a fanciful story, or telling a bold faced lie? We know by now that He was telling the truth. Let's just look at a few Scriptures to prove our point (Matthew 3:17; 12:8; 17:5; John 1:14).

Next, we see Jesus in Matthew 26:64 pronounce that He would sit at the right hand of the Power and come on the clouds of heaven. This is an illusion to Daniel 7:13. Is Jesus mad, crazy or insane? He would have had to be off His rocker to set Himself up for the abuse that was to come based on His own confession. The story of clouds and sitting with God, well that would be far fetched if He wasn't who He said He was. The high-priest's reactions are quite telling. Mad men, as we could note in Mark 5, are sent to live in caves. The high-priest doesn't send him away, he tears his clothes and loses it. He passes judgment on Him and they begin to spit, beat and strike Him. Let me declare plainly what you already know. He was not a liar or a lunatic. Jesus Christ, the Son of the living God, is Lord (John 8:14-18)!

Who do you know, who has reduced Jesus Christ to something less than the Bible proclaims Him to be? Their claim will most likely align with a perspective in Lewis' quote. Look for ways to listen to this person to share the good news that He is not a liar or lunatic. With compassion and humility, proclaim Jesus as Lord!

Time to Reflect

Scripture: Matthew 26:57-68

Observation: What are some of your thoughts about today's devotion?

Application: In what ways will the C.S. Lewis quote and our scripture help you to proclaim Christ to others?

Prayer: Pray about any <u>one</u> of the suggested options below. You are not expected to do all three unless the Holy Spirit directs you otherwise.

What can you commit to the Lord Jesus?
What do you want Him to do for you?
What do you want Him to help you to do?

Deeper Still: Using a good study Bible with commentary, review these passages concerning Christ's divinity: *John 1:18; 3:16, 35; 5:20; 5:32; Acts 3:13-15; 4:23-31.*

Praise and Worship: What praise or worship song comes to mind as you conclude our devotional for the day? I encourage you to listen to it now. Below is my playlist, which has a variety of artists and genres, so hold on and enjoy it if you care to partake.

"All Hail the Power of Jesus" – Bill & Gloria Gaither – Live[79]
"Crown Him with Many Crowns" – Michael W. Smith – 1995[80]
"Praise Medley" – CeCe Winans – Alone in His Presence[81]
"All Rise" – Babbie Mason[82]

---

[79] Bill and Gloria Gaither, "All Hail the Power of Jesus[Live]," provided by Gaither Music TV, September 27, 2012, YouTube music video, 3:23, https://www.youtube.com/watch?v=0m98RO7mkIE&list=RD0m98RO7mkIE&start_radio=1.

[80] Michael W. Smith, "Crown Him with Many Crowns," from the 1995 26th Annual GMA Dove Awards, uploaded by GMA Dove Awards, October 2, 2015, YouTube music video, 5:06, https://www.youtube.com/watch?v=Yd_u58cQpMI.

[81] CeCe Winans, "Praise Medley," uploaded by Kimjaydub1, December 7, 2011, YouTube music video, 5:02, https://www.youtube.com/watch?v=37RhBL2_6sY.

[82] Babbie Mason, "All Rise," provided by Curb Records, March 1, 2018, YouTube music video, 5:13, https://www.youtube.com/watch?v=gpBByw5OHD8.

SHINE THE LIGHT

Matthew 5:14–16

One of my godchildren's favorite pastimes is to get their flashlights out of the kitchen drawer, cut them on, get in the kitchen pantry and shut the door. It is dark in there and they just love it. Not because they love the dark, but because they have the flashlights. I pretend I don't know what happened to them and I call their names out loud as though I am searching for these little lost kids. When I finally open the door, they are shinning their lights at me and giggling their little heads off. They have such fun with the entire game and will look me straight in the eye once they are discovered, grab the doorknob and shut themselves in once again to repeat the process. Those flashlights are giving them light in a dark situation and they enjoy watching them light up that dark food pantry.

As we examine our scripture and this illustration, four principles resonate for us:

1. In Christ, we know where our light comes from. The kids know exactly where to find their flashlights. Scripture tells us exactly where we can find the light that we are to shine for a dark world. In John 8:12 we have the title that Jesus appropriates to Himself as the light of the world. As believers, we have the light of life because He is the light of men (John 1:4, 9).

2. In Christ, our light is turned on before we encounter the world. Did you notice? Once the kids get their flashlights, they turn them on <u>before</u> going into the dark pantry and shutting the door. In the Sermon on the Mount, Jesus pronounced that we are the light of the world (Matthew 5:14). Proverbs 4:18 says the path of the just is like the shining sun. As we are led on today's path, the light of Christ is a burning and shining lamp within us, just as it was for John the Baptist (John 5:35). We don't have to turn our lights on, they are already on. We just need to come into agreement with what the Word already says about the light within us.

3. In Christ, our light switch is always on. The kids never turn the flashlights off when they are in that dark pantry. Our light must always be on in this dark world. It is dangerous for us to think we can shut the light of God on and off in challenging situations and at will. Our light switch is not to be turned off for any reason. When we cut off our light, we may say something like, "I had to lay my religion down." When we become frustrated, irritated or aggravated with our surrounding circumstances, we should be like incandescent lights where we become brighter the harder things get. Light changes darkness, it does not become darkness. We are in Christ (2 Corinthians 5:17).

4. In Christ, our light gives light to all who encounter it and we have joy. As I appear to have discovered the kids in the pantry, with bright eyes and mischievous laughter, the kids turn their flashlights on me and crack up. This

is how we should be when our lights are shining so bright that our good works are glorifying the Father (Matt. 5:16) to individuals who encounter us.

5. Philippians 2:15 tells us that we shine as the lights in the world in a crooked and perverse generation. Those around us are looking for hope and light. We must radiate with the joy of Christ as we share the message of the Jesus (John 15:11).

6. In Christ, we are not afraid of the darkness because our light is not hidden or under a basket. Finally, those little rascals look me straight in the eye and close the door to the pantry, cracking up with excitement. They know they have the flashlights and they are not afraid of the dark. We face difficult and dark situations in our homes, families, jobs, communities and in relationships. People around us are facing health issues, financial problems, life-altering challenges and sinful situations. Our job is to be burning lanterns, illuminating the light of Jesus Christ (Ephesians 5:8) to show them the way.

Shining the light is living our life with spiritual impact before a Christ-less world. Will you allow your good works to glorify the Father today? In what ways can you radiate the light of Jesus today?

Scripture: Matthew 5:14-16

Observation: What are some of your thoughts about Christians being the light of the world and why is this important?

Application: Who needs your light of Christ to shine brightly? What good can they see so the Father in heaven is glorified?

Prayer: Pray about any <u>one</u> of the suggested options below. You are not expected to do all three unless the Holy Spirit directs you otherwise.

What can you commit to the Lord Jesus?
What do you want Him to do for you?
What do you want Him to help you to do?

Deeper Still: In Luke and Mark we find, "The Parable of the Revealed Light." If you go deeper today in your study, you will discover that when we illuminate and radiate a measure of light, our recompense is spiritual abundance. The scriptures clearly say, we are given more!

Using a good study Bible with commentary, review these passages concerning our light and works before the world. The parables: *Mark 4:21-25 and Luke 8:16-18.*

Praise and Worship: What praise or worship song comes to mind as you conclude our devotional for the day? I encourage you to listen to it now. Below is my playlist, which has a variety of artists and genres, so hold on and enjoy it if you care to partake.

"Shine the Light" – Babbie Mason[83]
"Standing In The Gap" – Babbie Mason[84]

---

83 Babbie Mason, "Shine the Light," provided by Universal Music Group, January 19, 2015, YouTube music video, https://www.youtube.com/watch?v=nVx32xGAYAs.

84 Babbie Mason, Standing In The Gap," provided by Curb Records, March 1, 2018, YouTube music video, 3:46, https://www.youtube.com/watch?v=Sf4FNlr6mx8.

JESUS IS THE ANSWER!

Ephesians 2:1-7

Our nation is in turmoil. Communities are in disarray. Marriages are breaking up. Children are fatherless and motherless due to abandonment, infidelity, rejection and abuse. There is domestic violence, sex-trafficking, gender identity confusion and same-sex attraction. We are sacrificing our children in the womb for a better way of life. Cancer, diabetes and HIV are epidemic. Sex has been turned into a recreational sport by our youth (and those not so youthful) devoid of the sacredness and meaning within the marriage bed. We are left with the spirits of lust, abandonment, rejection, jealousy, low self-esteem and no self-esteem. A world without Christ has lost its mind.

Israel was warned by the prophet Isaiah concerning times like these in which they called evil good and good evil; darkness was put for light and light was put for darkness, bitter for sweet and sweet for bitter. They were wise in their own eyes (Isaiah 5:20-21). Similarly, Paul outlined in Romans 1:18-32 the downward course we take in a life without Christ. Allow me to use a construction metaphor to explain. The foundation for a life <u>without</u> Christ is the practice of ungodliness (Romans 1:18-21). Ungodliness is cemented in the life of the nonbeliever. Ungodliness is not accepting or conforming to Jesus Christ. This foundation becomes rock solid because of the hardness of the heart. Upon this foundation a three-level house of unrighteousness is erected (Romans 1:22- 32). In the basement is the manifestation of uncleanness (Romans 1: 24-25). The first floor consists of vile passions (Romans 1:26-27) and the second floor is a debased mind (Romans 1:28-32). The debased mind is the opposite of pure and it opens the roof for all the mayhem we are experiencing.

Now that we understand the condition of the unconverted soul, there is a remedy. Ephesians 2:4-5 maps out the divine action of Christ toward us. It is the antidote for the ungodliness and unrighteousness that rages all around and in us. First, God is rich in mercy. Mercy is <u>not</u> receiving what we deserve. His boundless mercy is on display when He saves us. Second, God has great love with which He loved us (Romans 5:8). Third, we were dead in our trespasses, but He made us alive together with Christ. Fourth, by grace we are saved. Grace is receiving what we did not deserve. Can you feel the magnitude of His kindness, care, love and compassion for us? This may be a great place to shout–Hallelujah!

People all around us are hurting and looking for the answers to life, pain and suffering. They want to know if they matter to anyone. Why are they here? Does anyone love them for who they are? Can they find peace in all the chaos? Why does life hurt so badly?

We serve a compassionate Savior, "who raises us up... and made us sit together in the heavenly places in Christ Jesus, that in the ages to come He will show

the exceeding riches of His grace in His kindness toward us in Christ Jesus."
(Ephesians 2:6-7)

Would you look for the hurt and pain of someone around you today? Will you compassionately and lovingly tell them that Jesus is the answer to the sin of the world and the sin in their life? Are you willing to let them know that Jesus is who they are looking for? Will you share the ABCs of evangelism and invite them to **A**ccept, **B**elieve and **C**onfess Jesus Christ as their Lord and Savior? (Review the Romans Road scriptures on page xviii.)

Time to Reflect

Scripture: Ephesians 2:1-7

Observation: What are some of your thoughts about Jesus being the answer?

Application: What is too big for Jesus to change? Who needs you to bring them the answer?

Prayer: Pray about any <u>one</u> of the suggested options below. You are not expected to do all three unless the Holy Spirit directs you otherwise.

What can you commit to the Lord Jesus?
What do you want Him to do for you?
What do you want Him to help you to do?

Deeper Still: Using a good study Bible with commentary, review these passages concerning the mission of Christ: *Isa. 53; Matt. 5:17; 20:28; John 3:17; 10:10; 18:37.*

Praise and Worship: What praise or worship song comes to mind as you conclude our devotional for the day? I encourage you to listen to it now. Below is my playlist, which has a variety of artists and genres, so hold on and enjoy it if you care to partake.

"Jesus Is the Answer" – Brentwood Baptist–BeBe Winans[85]
"Is He Worthy" – Shane & Shane[86]
"Room at the Cross"– Clay Evans[87]
"Holy Forever" – Chris Tomlin – Lyric Video[88]

---

85 Brentwood Baptist, "Jesus Is the Answer," BeBe Winans' Surprise Performance of Jesus Is The Answer, uploaded by Brentwood Baptist, September 8, 2022, YouTube music video, 6:51, https://www.youtube.com/watch?v=WTJ3yzOxhmc.

86 Shane & Shane, "Is He Worthy," uploaded by Shane and Shane, February 11, 2019, YouTube music video, 4:53, https://www.youtube.com/watch?v=vEZzH-dWDOU.

87 Clay Evans, "Room at the Cross," uploaded by Garrison Bullier, November 17, 2009, YouTube music video, 4:25, https://www.youtube.com/watch?v=7xi8NF8eSRI.

88 Chris Tomlin, "Holy Forever (Lyric Video)," uploaded by christomlinmusic, July 15, 2022, YouTube music video, 5:08, https://www.youtube.com/watch?v=IkHgxKemCRk.

MAKE A DIFFERENCE

1 Peter 3:15-16

Like me, I am sure you've had at least one incident in your life when you were doing right, working for the glory of God and came up against slander, abuse, ridicule, false accusations, anger, wickedness and hatred. You probably had sleepless and tearful nights. Prayer and the Word became your weapons of choice. You had everyone you trusted praying for your way of escape. All the while, you were talking and wondering what went wrong. In fact, you firmly asserted that you did nothing wrong or deserving of this hostile situation.

Peter in our passage today says, 'Guess what? All of this is to be anticipated.' You will suffer when you do "good" toward others. It is unusual, but it happens. The question is, "How can we make a difference for Jesus Christ in tough times?" How can we stand steadfast and unmovable (1 Corinthians 15:58) in the face of unjust opposition? I love the Word of God because Peter tells us exactly how to make a difference for Christ in these types of situations.

Sanctify. In 1 Peter 3:15, Peter tells us first, to sanctify the Lord God in our hearts. Sanctify in the Greek refers to conducting this simple action in the future. In other words, when you encounter unfair opposition, dedicate yourself to God. Devote yourself to being morally pure. 1 Peter 3:10-11 provides five mandates that will help when suffering for what is right:

1.   Refrain your tongue from evil,

2.   Turn away from evil,

3.   Do good,

4.   Seek peace, and

5.   Pursue it (peace).

For this is a form of worshiping the Father "...in spirit and in truth..." (John 4:24).

Defend. Next, we must be ready to give a defense for what we believe with meekness and fear. The word fear here means to do so with a profound respect (yes, for the person who is not treating you fairly, justly or equally). Don't lose focus – we want our lives to make a difference in the lives of others. We must dare to stand and be different in the face of opposition. When we give a reason for the hope that is within us, we do it with boldness, humility and peacefulness. MacArthur says we must articulate what we believe humbly, thoughtfully, reasonably and biblically. (MacArthur, p. 1945) We don't hide, but we provide a logical, rational, compelling reason as to why we follow Jesus Christ. We invite the one who is inquiring about our hope to join us in our faith and Christian journey (1 Pet. 3:15).

Conscience. 1 Peter 3:16 implores us further to have a good conscience before our accusers. We belong to Christ. This means our conscience doesn't accuse us (Acts 24:16; 2 Cor. 1:12, 4:2). We don't have deep dark secrets of sin hidden from public view (2 Corinthians 4:2). We are not saying, "if they only knew." We submit ourselves under the regenerating and cleansing work of the Holy Spirit (Rom. 12:1-2; Heb. 9:14). When we have a good conscience, our conduct is always good, even when we are being reviled, falsely accused and mistreated.

Results. 1 Peter 3:16 demonstrates the outcome of deciding to make a difference God's way. Those who revile us will be ashamed. Romans 2:14-15 tells us that their conscience will accuse them. When we make a difference by following, growing and maturing in Jesus Christ, we can rest in the spiritual blessings found in 1 Peter 3:12. This verse encourages us that His eyes are on the righteous, His ears hear our prayers and His face (which means presence in the Greek) is against those who do evil.

Are you willing to make a difference in the lives of others even when they are the source of opposition and persecuting you? Can you list ways you can bless those who revile you? Ask God to give you the will to grant forgiveness and love in this situation. Pray earnestly for them to prosper. You will experience freedom, humility, peace and an increased sense of faith.

Scripture: 1 Peter 3:15-16

Observation: What are some of your thoughts about making a difference when facing persecution?

Application: What could you do to express the reason for the hope within you? What might you say?

Prayer: Pray about any <u>one</u> of the suggested options below. You are not expected to do all three unless the Holy Spirit directs you otherwise.

What can you commit to the Lord Jesus?
What do you want Him to do for you?
What do you want Him to help you to do?

Deeper Still: Using a good study Bible with commentary, review these passages concerning what it takes to make a difference in the face of opposition: *1 Pet. 3: 8-14; 2:23; Lev. 19:18; Prov. 20:22; Isa. 8:12-13; Matt. 18:35; 2 Tim. 2:15; Heb. 10:22.*

Praise and Worship: What praise or worship song comes to mind as you conclude our devotional for the day? I encourage you to listen to it now. Below is my playlist, which has a variety of artists and genres, so hold on and enjoy it if you care to partake.

"A Heart that Forgives" – Kevin Levar[89]
"Hills and Valleys (Acoustic Video)" – Tauen Wells[90]
"Whose Gonna Tell Them" – Marvin Winans[91]

---

[89] Kevin LeVar, "A Heart That Forgives," uploaded by Tee Bay, February 14, 2011, YouTube music video, 5:12, https://www.youtube.com/watch?v=8c-pr3PE7Dg

[90] Tauren Wells, "Hills and Valleys (Acoustic Video)," uploaded by Tauren Wells, January 20, 2017, YouTube music video, 4:11, https://www.youtube.com/watch?v=p4rRCjrAyCs.

[91] Marvin Winans, "Whose Gonna Tell Them," uploaded by Arima SDA Church, September 7, 2021, YouTube music video, 4:49, https://www.youtube.com/watch?v=1MalHvbSL5U.

WHY SOME BELIEVE AND SOME WILL NOT

John 8:44-45

Our love for Christ compels us to do His work in the great harvesting of souls as we encounter those within our circle of influence. I like to call this our private mission field. The people on this field can be the most challenging folks to reach, because often they think they have life (John 5:39). They profess to know Christ, because they can recall a time they walked down the aisle of the church and said they believe that Jesus is the Son of God. The challenge to this mere confession is that they possess no fruit (James 2:14). They are content with religious clichés and a worldly life style. They are firmly rooted in the world and desire everything except the risen Savior.

These individuals are easily identifiable on our mission field because they follow a religious Christian culture in language and some behaviors, but again, nothing in their life is yielded to Jesus Christ. They are quick to holler, "Don't judge me!" And you can often hear them say, "I don't see anything wrong with that or what I am doing." They live vicarious Christian lives based on the Christians they know. You may hear them say, "My father was a preacher." "My mother used to sing in the choir." "My grandmother was a missionary." You get the point. Their faith is tied to someone else, the name on the church they attend or their denomination.

My point is this: the Bible speaks of them as not having a true conversion experience (Titus 1:16; James 2:19-20). These individuals don't want to come on His terms and obedience is out of the question (1 John 2:3-6). They are led by their emotions and have no fruit because there are no true roots in Christ.

We are called to reach these individuals for Christ, too. One of the key things I have been asking myself as I encounter this religious spirit is, "How much of me am I willing to invest in this person?" Let's face it, they can be labor intensive. I have to ask myself: *Am I willing to disciple them one-on-one in the truth of the word? Am I comfortable with a fake confession because it is easier, even when I know their life doesn't remotely reflect a biblical conversion? What is God calling me to do with this person? How do I confront in a non-legalistic way and with the balance of grace, love and truth?*

I realize there are several things I can do with this individual: First, I must be willing to give of my time.

Second, I must be comfortable confronting them about their incongruent walk. In other words, their profession and their walk are not matching, and I love them enough to ask tough questions and to tell them in a loving yet truthful way about my observations. I can't take a part in assisting them in feeling safe and secure in their religious yet unconverted state. They will either separate from me or they will take heed as the Holy Spirit leads them. A key point is that I am in relationship with them and can have a courageous discussion about who they are in Christ. They can also challenge me about my walk – in fact, I make it a two-way street.

Third, I must stand on the Word of God. I must challenge them to get in the Word. Here is where I help them obtain good study tools and help facilitate the marking up of that brand-new study Bible I have recommended. I am prepared to seek the answers to their questions. I don't have to know all the answers, I explore the scriptures with them and we look for the answers they are seeking.

Fourth, I don't become a crutch for them. I have a limited amount of time and they must want to know more about Jesus. My job is to lovingly help them question their walk and faith.

Fifth, I must believe in the power of the Word and its ability to reach them as it reached me. The Holy Spirit is the one that will bring them into all truth, but I am to act as an ambassador for Christ. I must believe this is an easy thing for God and that there is no one too difficult for Christ. He saves to the uttermost, which means completely (Hebrews 7:25).

Sixth, throughout the process, I am serving, watching, listening, praying, fasting and crying out to God for their salvation and that the spirit of religion will be exposed. He is able and there is nothing too hard for Him. He saved me.

Finally, I must not neglect the call on my life to make disciples (Matt. 28:19). Even in the hardest situations, which may be my own mission field, making disciples is an investment of my time, energy and love. It is walking in obedience and manifesting the love of Christ. It is caring for those who are blind. It is releasing them to the Holy Spirit. It is knowing that when we have done all we can, it is not our job to save them but it is His.

Time to Reflect

Scripture: John 8:44-45

Observation: What are some of your thoughts about witnessing to those who are just religious?

Application: How would you demonstrate love, compassion and truth when talking with this person? Why is it important to hold a tension between these three?

Prayer: Pray about any <u>one</u> of the suggested options below. You are not expected to do all three unless the Holy Spirit directs you otherwise.

What can you commit to the Lord Jesus?
What do you want Him to do for you?
What do you want Him to help you to do?

Deeper Still: Using a good study Bible with commentary, review these passages: *James 2:19-20; Matt. 7:21; Mark 7:6; Luke 6:46; Gal. 5:6; 2 Tim. 3:5; 1 John 2:9; 3:8.*

Praise and Worship: What praise or worship song comes to mind as you conclude our devotional for the day? I encourage you to listen to it now. Below is my playlist, which has a variety of artists and genres, so hold on and enjoy it if you care to partake.

"Speak Lord" – Tata Vega[92]
"Love Lifted Me" – Benita Jones[93]
"Amazing" – Stephen Hurd[94]

---

[92] Tata Vega, "Speak Lord," provided by TuneCore, November 21, 2014, YouTube music video, 4:53, https://www.youtube.com/watch?v=Oy3FwUHA8kc

[93] Benita Jones, "Love Lifted Me," uploaded by Benita Jones, November 18, 2020, YouTube music video, 3:55, https://www.youtube.com/watch?v=psx8SD6aaTk.

[94] Stephen Hurd, "Amazing," provided by Absolute Marketing International Ltd, September 21, 2015, YouTube music video, 5:46, https://www.youtube.com/watch?v=07iW1GTABOA.

BLESSED ASSURANCE

1 Peter 1:3-5

When was the last time you thought you were sure of something, only to find you were wrong? Have you thought something was in one place in your home, only to discover it was in a totally different place? What about when you recall a place you visited: you believed it was on one street, only to find you grossly miscalculated and that vendor or store was two blocks over and one block down. Okay, perhaps this has only happened to me, but there are times when I can be so sure of something, only to find out in the end that my assurance, though free from doubt, was just plain wrong.

As we are compelled to go and tell others about Jesus Christ, we can be confident, without a shadow of doubt, that our faith claim of what Christ has done for us is the truth, the whole truth and nothing but the truth. We have a blessed assurance of an inheritance purchased by the precious blood of Jesus Christ (1 Peter 1:18-19).

I see six truths in our passage today, which can help those we are discipling to understand our faith more clearly. See if you caught them as you were reading the text:

1. **We Serve a Relational God**: Between the Father and the Son and among the believer and the Son, there is relationship. Let me explain and look carefully at 1 Peter 1:3. The Father is in divine relationship with the Son, Jesus Christ. Second, as believers we are in relationship with "our" Lord Jesus Christ. (John 5:17; 17:24- 26).

2. **We Serve a Merciful God**: Remember, mercy is receiving what you absolutely **do not** deserve. In other words, you are guilty of a crime, but the judge pardons you. 1 Peter 1:3 tells us that our God is abundant in mercy. Our God's mercy is great and extensive and pardons us from our sin (Eph. 2:4; Ps. 145:8).

3. **We Serve a God Who Saves**: The divine action of the Father and the sacrificial obedience of Jesus Christ provided redemption and salvation (John 3:3, 5; 1:13; 1 Pet 1:23). We are begotten into God's family (1 Peter 1:3). We serve a God who has given us a new family and a new nature (2 Corinthians 5:17).

4. **We Serve a Giving God**: In 1 Peter 1:4, we are assured of an inheritance. This is a sure inheritance that no one can claim but the individual believer. It is incorruptible – it is imperishable. It is undefiled – pure and free from stain. We may feel stained, but our inheritance is not. It does not fade away–unfading and undecaying. Our God gives us an inheritance. The uniqueness of Christianity is that our God provides for us now and for eternity. He is a good Father.

5. **We Serve a Sovereign God**: Our salvation is through a living hope, which comes through His plan of salvation to raise Jesus from the dead (1 Peter 1:3). According to the NKJV Study Bible, the hope we possess is not wishful. It is a dynamic confidence in our inheritance (Radmacher, 2007, p. 1981). He alone has made this possible for His children (John 3:16).

6. **We Serve a Faithful God**: 1 Peter 1:5 declares we are "...kept by the power of God through faith for salvation ..." Our gracious loving Father gives us saving faith (John 3:15; 5:24) and persevering faith (Matt. 24:13; Heb. 3:14).

Most Bibles that provide section headings entitle these verses as "A Heavenly Inheritance." We can only have this inheritance because of what Jesus Christ accomplished with His death, burial and resurrection. There is someone around you today that needs to know these truths and the blessed assurance you possess because of them. Who can you tell? How might you begin the conversation?

Scripture: 1 Peter 1:3-5

Observation: What other blessed assurances do you have in Christ?

Application: How can the six truths help you grow deeper in Christ?

Prayer: Pray about any <u>one</u> of the suggested options below. You are not expected to do all three unless the Holy Spirit directs you otherwise.

What can you commit to the Lord Jesus?
What do you want Him to do for you?
What do you want Him to help you to do?

Deeper Still: Using a good study Bible with commentary, review these passages concerning assurance in Christ: *John 6:40; 11:25; 12:46; Acts 13:39; 2 Cor. 6:1; Gal. 3:13-15; Eph. 2:8-9; 1 John 5:1.*

Praise and Worship: What praise or worship song comes to mind as you conclude our devotional for the day? I encourage you to listen to it now. Below is my playlist, which has a variety of artists and genres, so hold on and enjoy it if you care to partake.

"Blessed Assurance" – Shirley Caesar[95]
"My Hope Is Built" – Rev. Timothy Wright[96]
"Higher Ground" – Pastor E. Dewey Smith[97]
"His Mercy is More" – Keith & Kristyn Getty – Official Lyric Video[98]

---

[95] Shirley Caesar, "Blessed Assurance," provided by Curb Records, March 1, 2018, YouTube music video, 3:50, https://www.youtube.com/watch?v=inr1V8UJIUw

[96] Timothy Wright, My Hope Is Built," provided by Malaco Records, November 18, 2017, YouTube music video, 4:40, https://www.youtube.com/watch?v=qhA3xIehvJU

[97] Dewey Smith, Jr., "Higher Ground — Singing Old School Hymn," uploaded by BrothaRollins, December 17, 2010, YouTube music video, 6:49, https://www.youtube.com/watch?v=jqpo6iZNb2s.

[98] Keith & Kristyn Getty, Matt Boswell, Matt Papa Ft. Shane & Shane, "His Mercy is More (Live)," Live from the Sing! 2021 Conference, uploaded by KeithandKristyn Getty, May 20, 2022, YouTube music video, 4:01. https://www.youtube.com/watch?v=3mscAHe1UHE.

Week 5: Cling to the Savior!

"A Disciple of Christ Has a Growing Drive to Obey Regardless of the Consequences, Sacrifice, or Cost."
~Chuck Swindoll

MORE OF YOU, LORD, LESS OF ME

John 12:23-26

In the book of John, chapter 12 begins with Jesus being anointed for His burial. There is a plot to kill Lazarus, who He raised from the dead, and Jesus has triumphantly ridden into Jerusalem on a donkey with the crowd shouting, "Hosanna!" We are in what theologians call the Passion Week and only a short time away from Him hanging on the cross. In John 12:24, Jesus predicts and teaches His disciples about his suffering. As John 12:23-26 unfolds, Christ announces His hour has come. He is about to complete His main purpose for coming to dwell among us, and that is to give His life as a ransom (Mark 10:45).

As the Savior explains what is to become of Himself, He uses an agrarian example to illustrate His death and its results. A grain of wheat which abides alone will not reproduce, but a grain which falls to the ground plants and produces. Jesus was obedient unto death and the fruit of His death has multiplied throughout the centuries and has produced millions, if not billions, who believe in Jesus Christ.

We must be willing to die to ourselves in order that others will live. You might be thinking, "Hold on! I'm not willing to go that far." I would challenge you to evaluate what you truly believe. Christ's teaching on this topic is even more dogmatic in Matthew 10:37-39 and Luke 9:23-26. In fact, if using a Bible with section headings, you will find these passages entitled "Cost of Discipleship." The cost of discipleship is not a suggestion, but a response to the call to discipleship for every believer. It is one of the ways we can test the authenticity of our faith in Christ.

A true disciple of Christ desires more of Him and less of self. We are willing to die to ourselves, serve Him, suffer for His name and be wherever He is. We know that we are His hands, arms, ears, eyes and feet in the flesh. We are willing to go to the mission field and volunteer our time, talents and treasures freely. We live as stewards and not hoarding owners. Yes, and if necessary, we are even willing to physically die for our faith so that by our physical death, many would come to Christ. We are willing to pay the price because we understand the marvelous grace by which we are saved.

As we read Christ's teaching, we should have gnawing questions knocking at the door of our hearts: *What am I really willing to pay? Am I holding on to things that should be surrendered for His use?* It costs to follow Christ and it is this very clinging devotion to Christ that makes us infectious to the world around us.

Now this is a tall order, but it is necessary for others to live. It takes a commitment to cling and by this we mean to adhere, grip and hold on to the Master. Our hearts cry, as we die to ourselves, "Give me more of you, Lord, less of me."

Scripture: John 12:23-26

Observation: When it comes to more of Him and less of you, what is the desire of your heart?

Application: In what area of your life has Christ been asking you to die and you have been unwilling to yield? Who is not living a fruitful life around you because you won't cling to the Savior in obedience?

Prayer: Pray about any <u>one</u> of the suggested options below. You are not expected to do all three unless the Holy Spirit directs you otherwise.

What can you commit to the Lord Jesus?
What do you want Him to do for you?
What do you want Him to help you to do?

Deeper Still: Using a good study Bible with commentary, review these passages concerning an obedient life that cries for more of Christ: *Est. 4:16; Mark 8:35-36; John 15:16; Rom. 14:9; 1 Cor. 15:36; Eph. 5:1-2; Heb. 11:25; 1 Pet. 2:21.*

Praise and Worship: What praise or worship song comes to mind as you conclude our devotional for the day? I encourage you to listen to it now. Below is my playlist, which has a variety of artists and genres, so hold on and enjoy it if you care to partake.

"Whiter Than Snow" – Neville Peters[99]
"Goodbye to Me" – Damaris Carbaugh[100]
"I Am Not Ashamed of the Gospel" – The Brooklyn Tabernacle Choir[101]
"Old Rugged Cross" – Delores Winans[102]

---

[99] Neville Peters, "Whiter Than Snow," provided by TuneCore, May 3, 2018, YouTube music video, 4:18, https://www.youtube.com/watch?v=sXgCi5mhRYM.

[100] Damaris Carbaugh, "Goodbye to Me," provided by CDBaby, August 22, 2015, YouTube music video, 4:56, https://www.youtube.com/watch?v=ildD_TdijNY.

[101] The Brooklyn Tabernacle Choir, "I Am Not Ashamed of the Gospel," uploaded by Marcelo Barrera, July 5, 2013, YouTube music video, 5:53, https://www.youtube.com/watch?v=AStr4gfQGTM

[102] Delores Winans, "Old Rugged Cross," provided by Universal Music Group, September 25, 2014, YouTube music video, 4:15, https://www.youtube.com/watch?v=Hi03G_8KeFg.

MAKING MY ELECTION SURE

2 Peter 1:10

When the Bible speaks about election, it is referring to the sovereign act of God in saving us. There is a theological tension between the doctrines of Free Will and Election. The Bible teaches both and I am not attempting to enter this hotly debated theological conundrum today. It is enough to know for our purposes today that in the Sovereign will of God, He has chosen us.

As we walk this Christian walk, 2 Pet. 1:10 says, "Therefore, brethren, be even more diligent to make your call and election sure, for if you do these things you will never stumble." This is strong language–never stumble. It's right here in the text. We can validate our election by how we cling to the Savior and live our lives before the audience of the one Lord and Savior, Jesus Christ (Colossians 3:23).

When we go back to 2 Peter 1:5, we find Peter has outlined eight virtues, which help us grow, mature and bear much fruit in Christ. As you read through Peter's list, stop at each virtue and rate your <u>behavior</u> on a scale from 1-5. Then rate your <u>attitude</u>, and by attitude, we mean what you think or feel about the virtue. Be brutally honest with yourself as you examine the Greek meaning of the words in the context of 2 Peter 1:5- 8.

Election Sure Assessment

FAITH (Greek. Pistis)
Assurance or guarantee (Vine W. E.)

My behavior when it comes to Faith
☐ 1 – Little to no interest
☐ 2 – Need to work on
☐ 3 – Better than last year
☐ 4 – I see much growth
☐ 5 – Consistent and settled, I stumble very little in this area

My feelings or thoughts on Faith
☐ 1 – I am not interested and don't feel this is necessary
☐ 2 – It is too hard
☐ 3 – Depends on the day or situation
☐ 4 – My heart breaks for my sinful beliefs or stubborn feelings in this area
☐ 5 – My heart cries, "Take me deeper, Lord"

_____
_____
_____

VIRTUE (Greek. arete)
Moral excellence; moral goodness; excellence of character (Vine W. E.)

My behavior when it comes to Virtue
☐ 1 – Little to no interest
☐ 2 – Need to work on
☐ 3 – Better than last year
☐ 4 – I see much growth
☐ 5 – Consistent and settled, I stumble very little in this area

My feelings or thoughts on Virtue
☐ 1 – I am not interested and don't feel this is necessary
☐ 2 – It is too hard
☐ 3 – Depends on the day or situation
☐ 4 – My heart breaks for my sinful beliefs or stubborn feelings in this area
☐ 5 – My heart cries, "Take me deeper, Lord"

_____
_____
_____

KNOWLEDGE (Greek. gnosis)
Understand; recognize; to come to know (Vine W. E.)

My behavior when it comes to Knowledge
- ☐ 1 – Little to no interest
- ☐ 2 – Need to work on
- ☐ 3 – Better than last year
- ☐ 4 – I see much growth
- ☐ 5 – Consistent and settled, I stumble very little in this area

My feelings or thoughts on Knowledge
- ☐ 1 – I am not interested and don't feel this is necessary
- ☐ 2 – It is too hard
- ☐ 3 – Depends on the day or situation
- ☐ 4 – My heart breaks for my sinful beliefs or stubborn feelings in this area
- ☐ 5 – My heart cries, "Take me deeper, Lord"

SELF-CONTROL (Greek. enkrateia)
Controlling power of the will under the operation of God; it is our response to what we learn and put in practice; mastery over; temperance (Vine W. E.)

My behavior when it comes to Self-Control
- ☐ 1 – Little to no interest
- ☐ 2 – Need to work on
- ☐ 3 – Better than last year
- ☐ 4 – I see much growth
- ☐ 5 – Consistent and settled, I stumble very little in this area

My feelings or thoughts on Self-Control
- ☐ 1 – I am not interested and don't feel this is necessary
- ☐ 2 – It is too hard
- ☐ 3 – Depends on the day or situation
- ☐ 4 – My heart breaks for my sinful beliefs or stubborn feelings in this area
- ☐ 5 – My heart cries, "Take me deeper, Lord"

PERSEVERANCE (Greek hypomone)
The capacity to hold out or bear up in the face of difficulty; patience; endurance; fortitude; steadfastness (Arndt)

My behavior when it comes to Perseverance
☐ 1 – Little to no interest
☐ 2 – Need to work on
☐ 3 – Better than last year
☐ 4 – I see much growth
☐ 5 – Consistent and settled, I stumble very little in this area

My feelings or thoughts on Perseverance
☐ 1 – I am not interested and don't feel this is necessary
☐ 2 – It is too hard
☐ 3 – Depends on the day or situation
☐ 4 – My heart breaks for my sinful beliefs or stubborn feelings in this area
☐ 5 – My heart cries, "Take me deeper, Lord"

_____
_____
_____

GODLINESS (Greek eusebeia)
Godward attitude; does that which is well pleasing to Him; devoutness; piety; reverence toward God (Vine W. E.)

My behavior when it comes to Godliness
☐ 1 – Little to no interest
☐ 2 – Need to work on
☐ 3 – Better than last year
☐ 4 – I see much growth
☐ 5 – Consistent and settled, I stumble very little in this area

My feelings or thoughts on Godliness
☐ 1 – I am not interested and don't feel this is necessary
☐ 2 – It is too hard
☐ 3 – Depends on the day or situation
☐ 4 – My heart breaks for my sinful beliefs or stubborn feelings in this area
☐ 5 – My heart cries, "Take me deeper, Lord"

_____
_____
_____

BROTHERLY KINDNESS (Greek philadelphia)
Used figuratively to refer to brotherly love between Christians united through their common status as children of God (Balz)

My behavior when it comes to Brotherly Kindness
- ☐ 1 – Little to no interest
- ☐ 2 – Need to work on
- ☐ 3 – Better than last year
- ☐ 4 – I see much growth
- ☐ 5 – Consistent and settled, I stumble very little in this area

My feelings or thoughts on Brotherly Kindness
- ☐ 1 – I am not interested and don't feel this is necessary
- ☐ 2 – It is too hard
- ☐ 3 – Depends on the day or situation
- ☐ 4 – My heart breaks for my sinful beliefs or stubborn feelings in this area
- ☐ 5 – My heart cries, "Take me deeper, Lord"

_____
_____
_____

LOVE (Greek agape)
The quality of warm regard for the interest in another; esteem; affection; regard; human love without indication of the person who is the object of interest. (Arndt)

My behavior when it comes to Love
- ☐ 1 – Little to no interest
- ☐ 2 – Need to work on
- ☐ 3 – Better than last year
- ☐ 4 – I see much growth
- ☐ 5 – Consistent and settled, I stumble very little in this area

My feelings or thoughts on Love
- ☐ 1 – I am not interested and don't feel this is necessary
- ☐ 2 – It is too hard
- ☐ 3 – Depends on the day or situation
- ☐ 4 – My heart breaks for my sinful beliefs or stubborn feelings in this area
- ☐ 5 – My heart cries, "Take me deeper, Lord"

_____
_____
_____

How did you do? Did you find areas that are deficient? Did you find areas in which you can celebrate growth? Did you notice how, in the passage, these all build on one another, or as Peter says, "add to …"? Peter indicates that when these virtues are ours, we won't be barren or unfruitful in the knowledge of our Lord Jesus Christ (2 Peter 1:8). When we are lacking in these virtues, we are shortsighted, blind and have forgotten the wonderful cleansing from our old sins (2 Peter 1:9). When we remember and grow in these things, Peter says we do not stumble. These virtues can't be done outside of His divine power in us (2 Peter 1:3). As we assess our fruit in these eight areas, we confirm our election to ourselves and we cling more closely to Jesus Christ.

Time to Reflect

Scripture: 2 Pet. 1:10

Observation: When these virtues are exercised in your life with greater consistency, how will you be more effective for Christ?

Application: Which area do you want to concentrate on for the next month? Who might you get to help you? You may want to consider providing a copy of this assessment to your mentor or accountability partner to rate you in each area. Compare your ratings, note differences and prayerfully grow. Reassess yourself in six months using the same process. There is a blank assessment on page 93. Caution! Fruit grows from the inside out and not from the outside in. What is the single most important thing you can do to nurture and cultivate your inner woman to grow?

Prayer: Pray about any <u>one</u> of the suggested options below. You are not expected to do all three unless the Holy Spirit directs you otherwise.

What can you commit to the Lord Jesus?
What do you want Him to do for you?
What do you want Him to help you to do?

Deeper Still: Using a good study Bible with commentary, review these passages: *2 Pet. 1:1-4; 2 Cor. 2:14-15.*

Praise and Worship: What praise or worship song comes to mind as you conclude our devotional for the day? I encourage you to listen to it now. Below is my playlist, which has a variety of artists and genres, so hold on and enjoy it if you care to partake.

"Pleasing" – The Brooklyn Tabernacle Choir[103]
"Amazing Grace (My Chains Are Gone)" – CeCe Winans[104]
"I Won't Go Back" – William McDowell – Reprise and Lyrics[105]

---

[103] The Brooklyn Tabernacle Choir, "Pleasing (Live Performance Video)," uploaded by The Brooklyn Tabernacle Choir, August 20, 2018, YouTube music video, 5:52, https://www.youtube.com/watch?v=h1c3m8mRb8g.

[104] CeCe Winans, "Amazing Grace (My Chains Are Gone)," uploaded by Marquis Robertson, April 9, 2022, YouTube music video, 5:02, https://www.youtube.com/watch?v=hjdAzMHZMng.

[105] William McDowell, "I Won't Go Back w/reprise and lyrics," uploaded by AnisaKilgore, December 7, 2012, YouTube music video, 8:01, https://www.youtube.com/watch?v=7ULYOuLOLWo.

BELIEVE

John 3:36; Rom. 10:14-17

My prayer for you as we conclude this devotional is …

1. I pray you have a newfound focus and commitment to Jesus Christ (1 Corinthians 2:22).

2. I pray you are standing firmer on Christ, your solid rock (Ps. 18:2; 62:6-9; Matt. 7:24-27).

3. I pray you are equipped and able to witness using the simple ABCs to evangelize and lead others to Accept, Believe and Confess Christ (Romans 10:9-10).

4. I pray each day of your life is lived for the glory of God (Colossians 3:17).

5. I pray you are more radiant with the indwelling of Christ, which is Christ in you, the hope of glory (Colossians 1:27).

6. I pray for exponential growth in your life as you find women to pour into what you now know about Jesus Christ (John 15:16).

7. I pray you will know how to share the internal biblical evidence for your belief in Christ.

8. I pray you will learn how to share the external evidence for your belief in Christ.

9. I pray most of all that you BELIEVE!

My dearest sister, Jesus Christ has a fresh, bold call and purpose for your life. He wants you to cling to Him above all else. He has three marvelous actions He wants infused and embedded in your daily walk as you work out your salvation (you work because you are saved, not to be saved) with fear and trembling (Philippians 2:12-13):

SHARE – Know what you believe and why you believe it and make disciples! (Matthew 28:18)

STAND – Behave and stand unashamed for Jesus Christ! (Romans 1:16)

STAY – Be in the presence of Jesus! (John 15:8)

Time to Reflect
_____

Scripture: John 3:36; Rom. 10:14-17

Observation: What are your final thoughts about the call on your life and the above prayer for your life?

Application: In what ways can you share, stand and stay?

Prayer: Pray about any <u>one</u> of the suggested options below. You are not expected to do all three unless the Holy Spirit directs you otherwise.

What can you commit to the Lord Jesus?
What do you want Him to do for you?
What do you want Him to help you to do?

Deeper Still: **Gospel Reading Challenge**–Using a good study Bible with commentary, make a personal commitment to read through the gospels in the next three months. There are a total of 89 chapters from *Matthew 1:1–John 21:25*. That's almost one chapter a day over a 90-day period. Highlight scriptures which validate how necessary it is to have Jesus Christ as your Lord and Savior.

Increase your ability to succeed in this reading challenge by reading with another sister. You and your friend may want to journal and share thoughts several times during the week about how you are learning and growing in the grace and knowledge of your Lord and Savior Jesus Christ *(2 Peter 3:18)*.

Christ is necessary in the life of a woman!

Praise and Worship: What praise or worship song comes to mind as you conclude our devotional for the day? I encourage you to listen to it now. Below is my playlist, which has a variety of artists and genres, so hold on and enjoy it if you care to partake.

"Seek Ye First"–Vanessa Burge Garner[106]
"The King Is Coming" – Gaither Vocal Band – Live[107]
"Revelation 19:1" – Stephen Hurd[108]
"Worthy The Lamb" Gaither Vocal Band – Live[109]

_____

[106] Vanessa Burge Garner, "Seek Ye First," provided by CDBaby, June 22, 2017, YouTube music video, 6:35, https://www.youtube.com/watch?v=YvAWIeck4Jc

[107] Gaither Vocal Band, "The King Is Coming [Live]," uploaded by Gaither Music TV, October 11, 2012, YouTube music video, 5:17, https://www.youtube.com/watch?v=EaYRmSKm98c.

[108] Stephen Hurd, "Revelation 19:1," provided by Absolute Marketing International Ltd, June 23, 2015, YouTube music video, 5:34, https://www.youtube.com/watch?v=GznxPzJahwc.

[109] Gaither Vocal Band, "Worthy The Lamb [Live]," uploaded by Gaither Music TV, August 23, 2012, YouTube music video, 5:20, https://www.youtube.com/watch?v=DI6fU9p8Ptc.

Resources

Election Sure Assessment

Instructions: Review 2 Peter 1:5 and notice the eight virtues, which help us grow, mature and bear much fruit in Christ. As you read through Peter's list, stop at each virtue and rate your behavior on a scale from 1-5. Then rate your attitude. By attitude, we mean what you think or feel about the virtue. Be brutally honest with yourself as you examine the Greek meaning of the words in the context of 2 Peter 1:5-8.

FAITH (Greek. Pistis)
Assurance or guarantee (Vine W. E.)

My behavior when it comes to Faith
☐ 1 – Little to no interest
☐ 2 – Need to work on
☐ 3 – Better than last year
☐ 4 – I see much growth
☐ 5 – Consistent and settled, I stumble very little in this area

My feelings or thoughts on Faith
☐ 1 – I am not interested and don't feel this is necessary
☐ 2 – It is too hard
• 3 – Depends on the day or situation
☐ 4 – My heart breaks for my sinful beliefs or stubborn feelings in this area
☐ 5 – My heart cries, "Take me deeper, Lord"

VIRTUE (Greek. arete)
Moral excellence; moral goodness; excellence of character (Vine W. E.)

My behavior when it comes to Virtue
☐ 1 – Little to no interest
☐ 2 – Need to work on
☐ 3 – Better than last year
☐ 4 – I see much growth
☐ 5 – Consistent and settled, I stumble very little in this area

My feelings or thoughts on Virtue
☐ 1 – I am not interested and don't feel this is necessary
☐ 2 – It is too hard
☐ 3 – Depends on the day or situation
☐ 4 – My heart breaks for my sinful beliefs or stubborn feelings in this area
☐ 5 – My heart cries, "Take me deeper, Lord"

KNOWLEDGE (Greek. gnosis)
Understand; recognize; to come to know (Vine W. E.)

My behavior when it comes to Knowledge
- ☐ 1 – Little to no interest
- ☐ 2 – Need to work on
- ☐ 3 – Better than last year
- ☐ 4 – I see much growth
- ☐ 5 – Consistent and settled, I stumble very little in this area

My feelings or thoughts on Knowledge
- ☐ 1 – I am not interested and don't feel this is necessary
- ☐ 2 – It is too hard
- ☐ 3 – Depends on the day or situation
- ☐ 4 – My heart breaks for my sinful beliefs or stubborn feelings in this area
- ☐ 5 – My heart cries, "Take me deeper, Lord"

SELF-CONTROL (Greek. enkrateia)
Controlling power of the will under the operation of God; it is our response to what we learn and put in practice; mastery over; temperance (Vine W. E.)

My behavior when it comes to Self-Control
- ☐ 1 – Little to no interest
- ☐ 2 – Need to work on
- ☐ 3 – Better than last year
- ☐ 4 – I see much growth
- ☐ 5 – Consistent and settled, I stumble very little in this area

My feelings or thoughts on Self-Control
- ☐ 1 – I am not interested and don't feel this is necessary
- ☐ 2 – It is too hard
- ☐ 3 – Depends on the day or situation
- ☐ 4 – My heart breaks for my sinful beliefs or stubborn feelings in this area
- ☐ 5 – My heart cries, "Take me deeper, Lord"

PERSEVERANCE (Greek hypomone)
The capacity to hold out or bear up in the face of difficulty; patience; endurance; fortitude; steadfastness (Arndt)

My behavior when it comes to Perseverance
☐ 1 – Little to no interest
☐ 2 – Need to work on
☐ 3 – Better than last year
☐ 4 – I see much growth
☐ 5 – Consistent and settled, I stumble very little in this area

My feelings or thoughts on Perseverance
☐ 1 – I am not interested and don't feel this is necessary
☐ 2 – It is too hard
☐ 3 – Depends on the day or situation
☐ 4 – My heart breaks for my sinful beliefs or stubborn feelings in this area
☐ 5 – My heart cries, "Take me deeper, Lord"

GODLINESS (Greek eusebeia)
Godward attitude; does that which is well pleasing to Him; devoutness; piety; reverence toward God (Vine W. E.)

My behavior when it comes to Godliness
☐ 1 – Little to no interest
☐ 2 – Need to work on
☐ 3 – Better than last year
☐ 4 – I see much growth
☐ 5 – Consistent and settled, I stumble very little in this area

My feelings or thoughts on Godliness
☐ 1 – I am not interested and don't feel this is necessary
☐ 2 – It is too hard
☐ 3 – Depends on the day or situation
☐ 4 – My heart breaks for my sinful beliefs or stubborn feelings in this area
☐ 5 – My heart cries, "Take me deeper, Lord"

BROTHERLY KINDNESS (Greek philadelphia)
Used figuratively to refer to brotherly love between Christians united through their common status as children of God (Balz)

My behavior when it comes to Brotherly Kindness
☐ 1 – Little to no interest
☐ 2 – Need to work on
☐ 3 – Better than last year
☐ 4 – I see much growth
☐ 5 – Consistent and settled, I stumble very little in this area

My feelings or thoughts on Brotherly Kindness
☐ 1 – I am not interested and don't feel this is necessary
☐ 2 – It is too hard
☐ 3 – Depends on the day or situation
☐ 4 – My heart breaks for my sinful beliefs or stubborn feelings in this area
☐ 5 – My heart cries, "Take me deeper, Lord"

LOVE (Greek agape)
The quality of warm regard for the interest in another; esteem; affection; regard; human love without indication of the person who is the object of interest. (Arndt)

My behavior when it comes to Love
☐ 1 – Little to no interest
☐ 2 – Need to work on
☐ 3 – Better than last year
☐ 4 – I see much growth
☐ 5 – Consistent and settled, I stumble very little in this area

My feelings or thoughts on Love
☐ 1 – I am not interested and don't feel this is necessary
☐ 2 – It is too hard
☐ 3 – Depends on the day or situation
☐ 4 – My heart breaks for my sinful beliefs or stubborn feelings in this area
☐ 5 – My heart cries, "Take me deeper, Lord"

REFERENCES

58 Bible verses about Following Jesus Christ - Knowing Jesus - Bible. (n.d.). Retrieved from Knowing Jesus: http://bible.knowing-jesus.com

Arndt, W. D. (2000). A Greek-English lexicon of the New Testament and other early Christian literature (3rd ed., p. 1039). Chicago, IL.

Arndt, W. D. (2000). A Greek-English lexicon of the New Testament and other early Christian literature (3rd ed., p. 6). Chicago, IL.

Balz, H. R. (1990). Exegetical Dictionary of the New Testament (Vol. 3, p. 424). Grand Rapids, MI.

Earl D. Radmacher, G. E. (2007). *NKJV Study Bible 2nd Edition*. Nswhville: Thomas Nelson.

Erickson, M. J. (2001). *The Concise Dictionary of Christian Theology*. Wheaton: Crossway Books.

Erickson, M. (2001). *The Concise Dictionary of Christian Theology, rev. ed*. Wheaton: Crossway Books.

Erickson, M. (2001). *The Concise Dictionary of Christian Theology. rev. ed*. Wheaton: Crossway Books.

Grenz, S. J. (1996). *Who Needs Theology?* Downers Grove: IVP Academic.

Lewis, C. (n.d.). C. S. *Lewis Quotes*. Retrieved from https://www.goodreads.com/quotes/6979-i-am-trying-here-to-prevent-anyone-saying-the-really

Lockyer, H. *All the Women of the Bible*. Grand Rapids: Zondervan.

Louw, J. P. (1996). Greek-English lexicon of the New Testament: based on semantic domains (electronic ed. of the 2nd edition., Vol. 1, p. 138). New York, New York.

MacArthur, J. (1997). *The John MacArthur Study Bible, page 1945*. Nashville: Word Publishing.

MacArthur, J. (1997). *The MacArthur Study Bible*. Nashville: Thomas Nelson.

MacArthur, J. (1997). *The MacArthur Study Bible NKJV*. Nashville: Thomas Nelson, Inc.

McDowell, J. (2017, September 5). What is Truth. (J. Parshall, Interviewer)

Radmacher, E. D. (2007). *NKJV Study Bible 2nd ed*. Nashville: Thomas Nelson, Inc.

Sharp, T. (2012, September 17). *How Far is Earth from the Sun?* Retrieved from Space.com: space.com

Strobel, L. (2016). The Case for Christ. In L. Strobel, *The Case for Christ* (pp. 253-276). Grand Rapids: Zondervan.

Strobel, L. (2013). The Case for Christ Study Guide. In L. Strobel, *The Case for Christ Study Guide* (p. 7). Grand Rapids: Zondervan.

Strobel, L. (2013). *The Case for Christ Study Guide.* Grand Rapids: Zondervan.

Thompson, F. C. (1983). *The Thompson Chain-Reference Study Bible.* Indianapolis: B.B. Kirkbride Bible Co., Inc.

Thompson, F. C. (1983). *The Thompson Chain-Reference Study Bible.* Indianapolis: B.B. Kirkbridge Bible Co., Inc.

Thompson, F. C. (1997). *The Thompson Chain-Reference Study Bible.* Indianapolis: B.B, Kirkbride Bible Co., Inc.

Vine, W. E. (n.d.). Vine's Complete Expository Dictionary of Old and New Testament Words (Vol. 2, pp. 272–273). Nashville, TN, 1996.

Vine, W. E. (1996). Vine's Complete Expository Dictionary of Old and New Testament Words (Vol. 2, p. 620). Nashville, TN.

Vine, W. E. (1996). Vine's Complete Expository Dictionary of Old and New Testament Words (Vol 2, pp. 661-662). Nashville, TN.

Vine, W. E. (1996). Vine's Complete Expository Dictionary of Old and New Testament Words (Vol. 2, p. 43). Nashville, TN.

MEDIA BIBLIOGRAPHY YOUTUBE

A

Arrington, Chuck. "Were It Not For Grace." Uploaded by Josiah Birai. May 24, 2021. YouTube music video, 4:38. https://www.youtube.com/watch?v=6qoAf72zVDs.

B

Brooklyn Tabernacle Choir. "Jesus Is Lyrics," Lyrics Videos. February 19, 201. YouTube music video, 4:23. https://www.youtube.com/watch?v=mWWNiNJ1Utk.

Barrett, Pat. "The Way (New Horizon) (Lyric Video)." Uploaded by Pat Barrett. April 13, 2018. YouTube music video, 4:19. https://www.youtube.com/watch?v=MOzsJlk8p6I.

Badu, Sonnie. "My Soul Says Yes (Official Live Recording)." Uploaded by Official Sonnie Badu TV. October 9, 2016. YouTube music video, 9:09. https://www.youtube.com/watch?v=_Vuw0o0CXLI.

Brentwood Baptist. "Jesus Is the Answer." BeBe Winans' Surprise Performance of Jesus Is The Answer. Uploaded by Brentwood Baptist. September 8, 2022. YouTube music video, 6:51. https://www.youtube.com/watch?v=WTJ3yzOxhmc.

C

Caesar, Shirley. "Blessed Assurance." Provided by Curb Records. March 1, 2018. YouTube music video, 3:50. https://www.youtube.com/watch?v=inr1V8UJlUw.

Carbaugh, Damaris. "Almighty, I Surrender." Provided by CDBaby. July 8, 2015. YouTube music video, 4:39. https://www.youtube.com/watch?v=wiQUmwOAl64.

Carbaugh, Damaris. "Friend of A Wounded Heart." Provided by CDBaby. July 24, 2015. YouTube music video, 4:46. https://www.youtube.com/watch?v=KvT6X8fpSGQ.

Carbaugh, Damaris. "Goodbye to Me." Provided by CDBaby. August 22, 2015. YouTube music video, 4:56. https://www.youtube.com/watch?v=ildD_TdijNY.

Carbaugh, Damaris. "He Has Forgiven Me." Provided by CDBaby. July 13, 2015. YouTube music video, 4:56. https://www.youtube.com/watch?v=i6L0N4i2W4Y.

Cobbs Leonard, Tasha. "God So Loved ft. We the Kingdom (Live) ft. We the Kingdom." Uploaded by Tasha Cobbs Leonard. October 23, 2020. YouTube music video, 7:07. https://www.youtube.com/watch?v=iVux5s-SWFc

Coleman, Frankie. "The Old Rugged Cross." Provided by CDBaby. November 5, 2015. YouTube music video, 11:09. https://www.youtube.com/watch?v=5wdfClYmapo.

Cooke, Sam. "Touch The Hem Of His Garment." With the Soul Stirrers. Provided by Universal Music Group. December 2, 2018. YouTubem u s i c video, 2:02. https://www.youtube.com/watch?v=NfhEE7NPVjY.

Crabb, Adam. "Cross Made the Difference." Provided by Daywind Records. May 16, 2019. YouTube music video, 5:05. https://www.youtube.com/watch?v=xDRFP1xBkf4.

Crouch, Andrae. "Jesus is the Answer." Uploaded by Walter Robinson Jr. January 13, 2015. YouTube music video, 4:59. https://www.youtube.com/watch?v=cKHpweGR7Bs.

Crouch, Andrae. "Through it All [Live]." Uploaded by Gaither Music TV. August 30, 2012. YouTube music video, 3:09. https://www.youtube.com/watch?v=xO5Qt2VQn4k&list=RDxO5Qt2VQn4k&start_radio=1&rv=xO5Qt2VQn4k&t=50.

Crowns, Casting. "The Well." Uploaded by FollowingHimToday. October 18, 2011. YouTube music video, 5:04. https://www.youtube.com/watch?v=bW5unzXXC0k.

D

Dulaney, Todd. "Victory Belongs to Jesus (Lyrics)." Uploaded by Song of Solomon Ministries. November 20, 2016. YouTube music video, 5:58. https://www.youtube.com/watch?v=IkASX8Fd1tE.

E

Evans, Clay. "Room at the Cross." Uploaded by Garrison Bullier. November 17, 2009. YouTube music video, 4:2. https://www.youtube.com/watch?v=7xi8NF8eSRI.

F

FWC Resurrection Choir. "Oh, the Blood Medley (FWC Resurrection Choir)." Uploaded by Hayden Mccallum. February 13, 2023. YouTube music video, 7:03. https://www.youtube.com/watch?v=_-IG7rNhGcA.

G

Gaither, Bill and Gloria. "All Hail the Power of Jesus [Live]." Provided by Gaither Music TV. September 27, 2012. YouTubemusic video, 3:23. https://www.youtube.com/watch?v=0m98RO7mkIE&list=RD0m98RO7mkIE&start_radio=1.

Gaither Vocal Band, Michael English. "Please Forgive Me [Live]." Uploaded by Gaither Music TV. August 16, 2012. YouTube music video, 5:07. https://www.youtube.com/watch?v=aGW1x_lLp2o.

Gaither Vocal Band. "I Believe In A Hill Called Mount Calvary (Live)." Uploaded by Gaither Music TV. November 8, 2012. YouTube music video, 3:45. https://www.youtube.com/watch?v=4NSdy2N7mHA.

Gaither Vocal Band. "I Believe In A Hill Called Mount Calvary (Live/Lyric Video)." Uploaded by Gaither Music TV. May 26, 2017. YouTube music video, 3:45. https://www.youtube.com/watch?v=66Qq6yjFEBA.

Gaither Vocal Band. "The King Is Coming [Live]." Uploaded by Gaither Music TV. October 11, 2012. YouTube music video, 5:17. https://www.youtube.com/watch?v=EaYRmSKm98c.

Gaither Vocal Band. "There Is Something About That Name [Live]." Uploaded by Gaither Music TV. August 23, 2012. YouTube music video, 4:58. https://www.youtube.com/watch?v=SdSl9ynS3G4.

Gaither Vocal Band. "Worthy The Lamb [Live]." Uploaded by Gaither Music TV. August 23, 2012. YouTube music video, 5:20. https://www.youtube.com/watch?v=Dl6fU9p8Ptc.

Garner Burge, Vanessa. "Faith." Provided by CDBaby. June 22, 2017. YouTube music video, 5:10. https://www.youtube.com/watch?v=TyLQ5fQ_LK8.

Garner Burge, Vanessa. "Gratitude." Provided by CDBaby. June 22, 2017. YouTube music video, 4:30. https://www.youtube.com/watch?v=QvJ4i-Vlx1k.

Garner Burge, Vanessa. "I Know That Jesus Loves Me." Provided by CDBaby. June 22, 2017. YouTube music video, 4:16. https://www.youtube.com/watch?v=P8WR6vJEAx4.

Garner Burge, Vanessa. "Seek Ye First." Provided by CDBaby. June 22, 2017. YouTube music video, 6:35. https://www.youtube.com/watch?v=YvAWIeck4Jc .

Getty, Keith & Kristyn. "Come Thou Almighty King (Live from Sing! '21)." Uploaded by Keith and Kristyn Getty. April 19, 2022. YouTube music video, 3:31. https://www.youtube.com/watch?v=NT4IvKk8Yko.

Getty, Keith & Kristyn. "We Believe Apostle's Creed Lyric." Uploaded by Trinity Fellowship. January 16, 2017. YouTube music video, 4:50. https://www.youtube.com/watch?v=vZqX13gEbCM.

H

Hammond, Fred. "Bread of Heaven [lyrics]." Uploaded by ChristianFellowship5. August 26, 2009. YouTube music video, 5:01. https://www.youtube.com/watch?v=kjVgm9-XTqQ.

Hawkins, Walter. "Marvelous." Provided by Tune Core. June 19, 2014. Walter Hawkins and the Love Center Choir Love Alive V 25th Anniversary Reunion CD. YouTube music video, 7:36. https://www.youtube.com/watch?v=t4aIFXpgTyE.

Hurd, Stephen. "Amazing." Provided by Absolute Marketing International Ltd. September 21, 2015. YouTube music video, 5:46. https://www.youtube.com/watch?v=07iW1GTABOA.

Hurd, Stephen. "Revelation 19:1." Provided by Absolute Marketing International Ltd. June 23, 2015. YouTube music video, 5:34. https://www.youtube.com/watch?v=GznxPzJahwc.

I

Irving, Fleetwood. "Real (Jesus is Real to Me)." Uploaded by Deborrah Ogan. January 22, 201. YouTube music video, 3:01. https://www.youtube.com/watch?v=RzKxBHwPE_s.

J

Jeshke, Mark. "Trinity Hymn (Lyric Video)." Provided by Mark Jeschke. April 20, 2022. YouTube music video, 5:11. https://www.youtube.com/watch?v=MbOG8oN2G8E.

Jones, Benita. "Love Lifted Me." Uploaded by Benita Jones. November 18, 2020. YouTube music video, 3:55. https://www.youtube.com/watch?v=psx8SD6aaTk.

K

Kendrick, Graham. "Knowing You–Worship Song by Graham Kendrick from Philippians 3." Uploaded by Graham Kendrick Music. March 21, 2019. YouTube Music Video, 4:43. https://www.youtube.com/watch?v=4r8XfE_VNb0.

Keith & Kristyn Getty, Matt Boswell, Matt Papa Ft. Shane & Shane. "His Mercy is More Live." Live from the Sing! 2021 Conference. Uploaded by KeithandKristyn Getty. May 20, 2022. YouTube music video, 4:01. https://www.youtube.com/watch?v=3mscAHe1UHE.

Keith & Kristyn Getty Ft. Chris Tomlin. "Is He Worthy? (Live from Sing! '21)." Uploaded by Keith and Kristyn Getty. April 8, 2022. YouTube music video, 4:37. https://www.youtube.com/watch?v=As77j073jxM.

Kenoly, Ron. "Oh the Glory of Your Presence [Live]." Provided by Absolute Marketing International Ltd. June 23, 2015. YouTube music video, 4:37. https://www.youtube.com/watch?v=F4TYwm4aQ4U.

L

Larson, Grace. "Wonderful, Merciful Savior." Uploaded by Bryan Bryan T, Family Worship Center in Baton Rouge, LA. April 30, 2017. YouTube music video, 7:48. https://www.youtube.com/watch?v=AFIAeNKyBoo.

Larson, Joseph. "Holy, Holy, Holy." Provided by TuneCore. May 19, 2015. YouTube music video, 7:55. https://www.youtube.com/watch?v=cpNulfUCVZc.

Larson, Joseph. "It's My Desire (Live)." Provided to YouTube by TuneCore. May 19, 2015. YouTube music video, 6:45. https://www.youtube.com/watch?v=halzlop2hps.

LeVar, Kevin. "A Heart That Forgives." Uploaded by Tee Bay. February 14, 2011. YouTube music video, 5:12. https://www.youtube.com/watch?v=8c-pr3PE7Dg.

Lockridge, S.M. "That's My King." Uploaded by Albert Martin. July 23, 2008. YouTube sermon video, 3:18. https://www.youtube.com/watch?v=yzqTFNfeDnE.

M

Maranatha! Music. "Lord I Lift Your Name on High (Lyric Video)." Uploaded by Maranatha! Music. March 30, 2016. YouTube music video, 4:23. https://www.youtube.com/watch?v=tQiapzfQoq0.

Maranatha! Music. "Maranatha Singers–Thy Word [with lyrics]." Uploaded by Worship Videos. August 24, 2015. YouTube music video, 3:33. https://www.youtube.com/watch?v=npWJZwgmKMo.

Maranatha Singers. "He Knows My Name." Uploaded by Julz P. March 16, 2007. YouTube music video, 3:25. https://www.youtube.com/watch?v=hXsiWoyjw60.

Marshall Hall, Angela Primm, Jason Crabb. "Take My Hand, Precious Lord (Live)." Uploaded by Gaither Music TV. July 11, 2012. YouTube music video, 6:37. https://www.youtube.com/watch?v=RaF16IlysQc.

Mason, Babbie. "All Rise." Provided by Cur. Records. March 1, 2018. YouTube music video, 5:13. https://www.youtube.com/watch?v=gpBByw5OHD8.

Mason, Babbie. "Shine the Light." Provided by Universal Music Group. January 19, 2015. YouTube music video, 4:03. https://www.youtube.com/watch?v=nVx32xGAYAs.

Mason, Babbie. "Standing In The Gap." Provided by Curb Records. March 1, 2018. YouTube music video, 3:46. https://www.youtube.com/watch?v=Sf4FNlr6mx8.

Mason, Babbie. "What Can Separate you?" Uploaded by Al Bums. April 18, 2017. YouTube music video, 4:42. https://www.youtube.com/watch?v=PMCn3HEIAX0.

McDowell, William. "I Won't Go Back w/reprise and lyrics." Uploaded by AnisaKilgore. December 7, 2012. YouTube music video, 8:01. https://www.youtube.com/watch?v=7ULYouL0LWo.

Mississippi Mass Choir. "How Excellent." Uploaded by Kleavell20. June 4, 2012. YouTube music video, 5:28. https://www.youtube.com/watch?v=W17-4LDYH74.

Moen, Don. "Give Thanks Live Worship Sessions." Uploaded by Don Moen TV. July 26, 2017. YouTube music video, 4:23. https://www.youtube.com/watch?v=blbslHDgceY.

Moen, Don. "Grace Greater Than Our Sin." Uploaded by Don Moen TV. June 2, 2017. YouTube music video, 3:19. https://www.youtube.com/watch?v=xdUDqKIIQxM.

Moen, Don. "No Other Name." Uploaded by The Watchers Worship. January 21, 2016. YouTube music video, 4:12. https://www.youtube.com/watch?v=z40TLeD3_mo.

Moore, Chandler. "King of Kings: Official Music Video." Uploaded by Essential Worship. March 3, 2021. YouTube music Video, 4:20. https://www.youtube.com/watch?v=09azEfx71rc.

N

Nelson, Jonathan. "I Believe (Island Medley) (So Long Bye Bye) (Radio Edit)." Provided by Entertainment One Distribution US. May 1, 2016. YouTube music video, 4:00. https://www.youtube.com/watch?v=LUCN0G5dtf0.

P

Peters, Neville. "Whiter Than Snow." Provided by TuneCore. May 3, 2018. YouTube music video, 4:18. https://www.youtube.com/watch?v=sXgCi5mhRYM.

Phelps, David. "You Are My All In All/Canon in D (Live)." Uploaded by Gaither Music TV. November 22, 2012. YouTube music video, 5:13. https://www.youtube.com/watch?v=OLilYpRAuU4.

Phipps, Wintley. "His Truth Is Marching On." Uploaded by Gabriel J Melo. October 19, 2019. YouTube music video, 4:24. https://www.youtube.com/watch?v=27stW_-mV_E.

Penrod, Guy. "Because He Lives." Uploaded by Gateway Church TV. November 23, 2017. YouTube music video, 3:37. https://www.youtube.com/watch?v=V2P57HSVzqc.

Primm, Angie. "Fill My Cup, Lord (Live)." Provided by Gaither Music TV. February 7, 2013. YouTube music video, 3:46. https://www.youtube.com/watch?v=_8ykaEdfiZ4.

R

Randle, Lynda. "Have Thine Own Way." Provided by Universal Music Group. July 29, 2018. YouTube music video, 3:12. https://www.youtube.com/watch?v=FKldMtr08FE.

Richards, Noel. "I Really Want to Worship You My Lord." Uploaded by WeAreWorship Lyrics & Chords. March 21, 2017. YouTube music video, 4:38. https://www.youtube.com/watch?v=URIkXQfHUBc.

S

Shane & Shane. "In Christ Alone." Provided by Catapult Reservatory, LLC. August 28, 2018. YouTube music video, 4:36. https://www.youtube.com/watch?v=aLOsM3ON-24.

Shane & Shane. "Is He Worthy." Uploaded by Shane and Shane. February 11, 2019. YouTube music video, 4:53. https://www.youtube.com/watch?v=vEZzH-dWDOU.

Slaughter, Alvin. "He Is Lord." Provided by Absolute Marketing International Ltd. September 21, 2015. YouTube music video, 3:07. https://www.youtube.com/watch?v=25KQeFYqhJU.

Slaughter, Alvin. "I Will Run to You." Uploaded by awayclouds. July 27, 2009. YouTube music video, 9:50. https://www.youtube.com/watch?v=jnfy9NcjAkU.

Smith, E. Dewey Jr., "Higher Ground – Singing Old School Hymn." Uploaded by BrothaRollins. December 17, 2010. YouTube music video, 6:49. https://www.youtube.com/watch?v=jqpo6iZNb2s.

Smith, Michael W. "Crown Him with Many Crowns." from the 1995 26th Annual GMA Dove Awards. Uploaded by GMA Dove Awards. October 2, 2015. YouTube music video, 5:06. https://www.youtube.com/watch?v=Yd_u58cQpMI.

SoulJa Of God. The True Story Behind The Song "I Have Decided To Follow Jesus." Uploaded by SoulJa Of God. April 29, 2017. YouTube music video, 5:23. https://www.youtube.com/watch?v=9mLC2XAXKac.

Strobel, Lee. "The Case for Christ." Uploaded by Passion City Church. July 1, 2018. YouTube conference video, 39:52. https://www.youtube.com/watch?v=67uj2qvQi_k.

Strobel, Lee. "The Case for Christ Documentary." Uploaded by ChannelC2. November 13, 2021. YouTube video, 1:11:26. https://www.youtube.com/results?search_query=the+case+for+christ+lee+strobel+documentary.

Sovereign Grace Music. "All I Have Is Christ (feat. Paul Baloche) – Official Lyric Video." Uploaded by Sovereign Grace Music. April 21, 2014. YouTube music video, 5:17. https://www.youtube.com/watch?v=ugGucoYMmKg.

Sovereign Grace Music. "Jesus, There's No One Like You – Prayers of the Saints Live." Uploaded by ChaNel Lyric Videos. April 14, 2021. YouTube music video, 4:26. https://www.youtube.com/watch?v=9kjqMKFgfo0.

Sovereign Grace Music. "O Lord My Rock and My Redeemer – T4G Live IV [Official Lyric Video]." Uploaded by Sovereign Grace Music. March 31, 2020. YouTube music video, 5:18. https://www.youtube.com/watch?v=TxC16duiHvQ.

T

The Brooklyn Tabernacle Choir. "He's Been Faithful." Uploaded by Marcelo Barrera. January 29, 2017. YouTube music video, 5:26. https://www.youtube.com/watch?v=ymiZ2xB-AfU.

The Brooklyn Tabernacle Choir. "I Am Not Ashamed of the Gospel." Uploaded by Marcelo Barrera. July 5, 2013. YouTube music video, 5:53. https://www.youtube.com/watch?v=AStr4gfQGTM.

The Brooklyn Tabernacle Choir. "Jesus I Love You (Live)." Provided by TuneCore. October 10, 2019. YouTube music video, 6:20. https://www.youtube.com/watch?v=QdEOUWoELhs.

The Brooklyn Tabernacle Choir. "Pleasing (Live Performance Video)." Uploaded by The Brooklyn Tabernacle Choir. August 20, 2018. YouTube music video, 5:52. https://www.youtube.com/watch?v=h1c3m8mRb8g.

The O'Neal Twins. "Jesus Dropped The Charges." Provided by Malaco Records. June 27, 2018. YouTube music video, 7:49. https://www.youtube.com/watch?v=QhMvvW5qvxc.

The Shiloh Church Choir. "Behold Our God [Lyric Video]." Sovereign Grace Music together with The Shiloh Church Choir. Uploaded by Sovereign Grace Music. October 29, 2019. YouTube music video, 6:50. https://www.youtube.com/watch?v=lIUGUPEopbI.

Tomlin, Chris. "Come Thou Fount (I Will Sing)." Provided by Universal Music Group. July 24, 2018. YouTube music video, 4:59. https://www.youtube.com/watch?v=9OIusL_X8Jw.

Tomlin, Chris. "Holy Forever (Lyric Video)." Uploaded by christomlinmusic. July 15, 2022. YouTube music video, 5:08. https://www.youtube.com/watch?v=IkHgxKemCRk.

Tomlin, Chris. "Is He Worthy? (Live)." Uploaded by Chris Tomlin Music, Official Live Video. February 1, 2019. YouTube music video, 6:56. https://www.youtube.com/watch?v=FkRiYsTN7KY.

V

Vega, Tata. "Oh It Is Jesus." Provided by Rhino/Warner Records. January 23, 2017. YouTube music video, 5:04. https://www.youtube.com/watch?v=lBHTd5XtNIM.

Vega, Tata. "Speak Lord." Provided by TuneCore. November 21, 2014. YouTube music video, 4:53. https://www.youtube.com/watch?v=Oy3FwUHA8kc.

W

"Walk in the Light." Uploaded by Charles Pope. April 2, 2011. YouTube music video, 5:42. https://www.youtube.com/watch?v=GCTR0WXZjwk.

Walker, Lydia. "I Have Decided to Follow Jesus (Lyric Video)." Uploaded by Lydia Walker. August 11, 2021. YouTube music video, 2:45. https://www.youtube.com/watch?v=L7XHeCZB5KU.

Wells, Tauren. "Hills and Valleys (Acoustic Video)." Uploaded by Tauren Wells. January 20, 2017. YouTube music video, 4:11. https://www.youtube.com/watch?v=p4rRCjrAyCs.

Winans, CeCe. "Amazing Grace (My Chains Are Gone)." Uploaded by Marquis Robertson. April 9, 2022. YouTube music video, 5:02. https://www.youtube.com/watch?v=hjdAzMHZMng.

Winans, CeCe. "Jesus, You're Beautiful (Official Audio)." Uploaded by CeCe Winans. March 12, 2021. YouTube music video, 7:13. https://www.youtube.com/watch?v=daWu1MBbx5M.

Winans, CeCe. "Praise Medley." Uploaded by Kimjaydub1. December 7, 2011. YouTube music video, 5:02. https://www.youtube.com/watch?v=37RhBL2_6sY.

Winans, CeCe. "The Blood/Because He Lives." Uploaded by Marquis Robertson. April 14, 2020. YouTube music video, 4:30. https://www.youtube.com/watch?v=ZwByK7XPwHI.

Winans, CeCe. "Worthy of it All (Official Audio)." Uploaded by CeCe Winans. March 12, 2021. YouTube music video, 5:28. https://www.youtube.com/watch?v=JzZSrOPeolc.

Winans, Delores. "Old Rugged Cross," Provided by Universal Music Group. September 25, 2014. YouTube music video, 4:15. https://www.youtube.com/watch?v=Hi03G_8KeFg.

Winans, Marvin. "Whose Gonna Tell Them." Uploaded by Arima SDA Church. September 7, 2021. YouTube music video, 4:49. https://www.youtube.com/watch?v=1MalHvbSL5U.

Wright, Timothy. "My Hope Is Built." Provided by Malaco Records. November 18, 2017. YouTube music video, 4:40. https://www.youtube.com/watch?v=qhA3xIehvJU.

NOTES

NOTES

74654506R00066